An Examination of Characters and Spaces in Film
Narratives in the Context of Panopticon and Chronotope
within the Framework of Narratology Theory

Berceste Gülçin Özdemir

An Examination of Characters and Spaces in Film Narratives in the Context of Panopticon and Chronotope within the Framework of Narratology Theory

Bibliographic Information published by the Deutsche Nationalbibliothek
The Deutsche Nationalbibliothek lists this publication in the Deutsche Nationalbibliografie; detailed bibliographic data is available in the internet at http://dnb.d-nb.de.

ISBN 978-3-631-78596-6 (Print)
E-ISBN 978-3-651-78702-1 (E-PDF)
E-ISBN 978-3-631-78703-8 (EPUB)
E-ISBN 978-3-631-78704-5 (MOBI)
DOI 10.3726/b15500

© Peter Lang GmbH
Internationaler Verlag der Wissenschaften
Berlin 2019
All rights reserved.

Peter Lang – Berlin · Bern · Bruxelles · New York ·
Oxford · Warszawa · Wien

All parts of this publication are protected by copyright. Any utilisation outside the strict limits of the copyright law, without the permission of the publisher, is forbidden and liable to prosecution. This applies in particular to reproductions, translations, microfilming, and storage and processing in electronic retrieval systems.

This publication has been peer reviewed.

www.peterlang.com

Abstract

Narratology began to be discussed in the academic literature in the 1960s when the theoreticians who were called 'the structuralists' explained their thoughts. After the 1960s, especially between 1980 and 1990, the theorists who revealed different approaches from structuralists are characterized as the post-classical period. Narratology, which is discussed in many areas, point to an interdisciplinary field of discussion. Narratology began with theories of literature and literary discussions, and cinema is one of the areas that discusses narratology. In the study, a short summary of the history of narratology will be provided and information will be given about how the basis of this field of study was shaped. This study aims at analyzing the characters and spaces in films (writing case studies) in the framework of the Theory of Narrative in the context of the concepts of panopticon and chronotope. In this regard, Mieke Bal's book *Narratology: Introduction to the Theory of Narrative* (1985) will be used as a basis for analyzing narratology in film narratives. The study took Koca Dünya (2016) and Dört Köşeli Üçgen (2018) as case studies, and the presentation of time element will be examined while trying to analyze basically how the characters and places are presented to the audience in terms of narratology in the film narrative. The concepts of panopticon and chronotope are the contexts that will support the process of making sense of this analysis. In examining the relation of spaces with the character, the questioning of Bal in which she associated the space to the character, and she questioned to whom space was presented make us think how space was experienced by the character and also the relationship between the space and the character in the narrative.

Key words: Narratology, film narrative, space, panopticon, chronotope.

Contents

Introduction 9

Essentials of Narratology 13

Narratology Elements in Film Narratives 23

The Elements of Space and Time in Film Narrative 29

Time and Space in the Film Narrative with Mieke Bal 35

Sense-Making Levels 39
   Film Reviews: Space and Time in the Koca Dünya
      Narrative in the Context of Chronotope 39
   The Story of the Film 39
   Film Review 40

Space and Time in the Dört Köşeli Üçgen Narrative
in the Context of Panopticon 63
   The Story of the Film 63
   Film Review 63

Conclusion 95

References 99

Introduction

Aristotle, who is one of the thinkers who are the source of the basic ideas of all sciences, has laid the foundations of narratology while expressing his important ideas on the art of poetry hundreds of years ago. Likewise, all the theorists working on narratology have a general opinion that Aristotle's *Poetika* is the basis of this science. According to Manfred Jahn, who is one of the theorists worked on narratology for many years, the roots of narratology are based on the distinction of mimesis and diegesis from Plato (428–348 BC) and Aristotle (384–322 BC), as in the Western theories of fiction (Jahn, 2015: 45).

Poetika makes it possible to come up with different thoughts about concepts like poetry, poet, story, etc. every time the reader reads it and prepares the reader for a journey to the historical origin of narratology before the narrative is told. At the same time, the work, which helps to reconsider the elements of the art of cinema, offers the thought path of an important thinker regarding the elements of film narratives. While expressing his thoughts on the art of poetry in his work *Poetika*, Aristotle also draws attention to the importance of this art as a literary product and states that new poetry types emerged in the writing of tragedies and comedies (Aristotle, 2011: 41). Tragedy presents data regarding the historical background of the theater and shows the processes of the development of acting. Likewise, characters, as well as stories, are among the most important elements of film narratives. According to Aristotle, tragedy is an imitation of an action. This action is represented by persons in action who should have certain characteristics with regard to character and thought. Thus, character and thought are the two actions of tragedy. People are happy or unhappy depending on the characters and thoughts in these actions. According to Aristotle, an imitation of an action is a story. The story is the fiction of the events, whereas the character is the characteristics of the persons who take the action. On the other hand, the thought is defined as the thing that is proved by the ones who engage in private speech. Aristotle says that tragedy has six elements and these elements reveal tragedy as a type of poetry. These six items are story, characters, language, thoughts, decoration, and music (Aristotle, 2011: 45).

Aristotle's thoughts on tragedy remind us of the basic elements of cinema. In film narratives, in which an action or a series of actions are formed as fiction, story, character, dialog, the discourse of the narrative, mise-en-scene, and music are parallel to the 6 elements that Aristotle said existed in the tragedy. The subject of this book consists of how the elements mentioned in narratology are formed in film narratives and what these elements present to the spectators. In this context, the elements that are given in case study films will be interpreted with the help of film reviews. While examining the characters and spaces in film narratives, the examination will be carried out within the framework of the concepts about which Mieke Bal commented in terms of narratology in her book *Narratology: Introduction to the Theory of Narrative* (1985). Within the context of the relation of spaces with characters, the concepts of interior and exterior spaces and how spaces are experienced by the characters which are among the concepts of Bal and within the context of the relation of the spaces with the story, the spaces where Bal distinguishes in terms of the manners of action of the characters and the concepts of steady space and dynamically functioning space will be examined in film analysis. From the point of view of narratology, Bal's thoughts are considered important among the theorists working on narratology after 1990. The reason that Bal's thoughts are used in this study is that these thoughts enable both the political and philosophical debates of narrative elements such as story, plot, and spectators. The concepts of panopticon and chronotope have also been used by film theorists in film analyses for many years. The meaning of these two concepts can provide multiple readings and enable the use of different perspectives in the context of film review. Bal's explanations about narratology allow more abstract film reviews and pave the way for drawing a thought path with a more philosophical approach. That is why, within the framework of the ideas of Bal, film reviews were carried out in the context of the concepts of panopticon and chronotope. One of the most important reasons for the selection of these concepts in terms of both films lies in the fact that the content of these concepts has parallel meanings with the topics and questioning that the films take to their focus centers.

Essentials of Narratology

> "The told story mentions the 'who' of the action. Then the identicalness of 'who' is a narrative identicalness" (Ricœur, 2016: 406).

The narrative is the stories that are presented to the spectator through narrative, fiction or reality-based events. The subject that is just as important as the content of the narrative is how the narrative is told. In this regard, concepts such as character, space, plot, time, spectator, location, story, cause-effect, events play an important role in the examination and interpretation of film narratives. According to Roland Barthes, the narrative is present at all times, in all places, and in all societies. The narrative began with the history of humanity and it is present among the peoples all over the world because each people certainly have their own narratives (Barthes, 2016: 101). Stating that literary works are symbolic, Barthes emphasizes that the symbol is not an image, but the plurality of meanings (Barthes, 2017: 44). In this respect, the same approach is reached when the thoughts of Barthes that he stated by referring to literary works are considered because the symbols that exist in every work of art gain meaning according to the interpretation system of those who read it.

In his book *Myth and Meaning* (1978), Claude Levi Strauss states that some narratives do not exist as written sources in their relationship with history and expresses that scientists can reach historical information through stories that people tell (Strauss, 2018: 57). As it is understood from the explanations of Strauss, narratives can sometimes differ when they reach people, whether they are written or not. Although symbols gain meaning according to the interpretation of those who read it, they can present more tangible data to the reader compared to the works which verbally reach humanity. According to Wayne C. Booth, narratology is an art, not a science, and there are systematic elements of every art (Booth, 2012: 176). Even Booth, who accepts narrative as art, has emphasized that a system must exist within an art. This system has been shaped over the years in the developmental process of narratology.

The analysis of the history of the narrative reveals the fact that songs, novels, poems, tales, stories, epics and many more types of narratives exist. The film narrative is one of the narratives that have the feature of reaching the spectators more within the existing narratives. Robert Kolker summarizes how the origin of film narratives was comprised by stating

"The origins of the basic narratives in films go back to renaissance comedy and nineteenth-century melodrama which are the stories of lost and re-demanded love, the women who were attacked by corrupt people, the families and other beloved institutions which greedy and despicable people endanger, the sanctity of home and the nuclear family order, the innocence of children, the patience of women and men's resolvable confusion" (Kolker, 2011: 269).

According to Susan Lanser, when the beginning of narrative poetics is dated back to ancient Greeks, Russian Formalists, Anglo-American New Critics or French Structuralists, the problems of gender are said to be outside the early distinctions or interests of the field. This is intended to determine the "classical" forms and universal laws of narrative theory and the essentials of formal typologies, and also to define the stylistic and structural elements which seem to be repeated in a very different way from thematic content, actual readers or in many cases cultural codes (Lanser, 2013: 2). As it is understood from the statements made by Lanser and Kolker regarding the history of the narrative, narratives may include cultural codes, may appear in different styles and include anomalous discourses from cultural codes.

In her reference to Robert Lapsley and Michael Westlake, Susan Hayward states that 'the narrative seems as natural as life' because it is found in many cultural forms. Stating that film narrative and narrative analyses have become a theoretical field of research in structuralist debates about cinema, Hayward indicates that tales and folklore narratives constitute important sources for film narratives. She states that Vladimir Propp's (the 1920s) work about the movement field of action in fairy tales and Claude Levi Strauss's (the 1950s) studies about the structure of folklore narratives are the outstanding works in this context. Hayward indicates that theorists who are interested in the structuralist approach nowadays benefit from the works of Gerard Genette (1980) who executed the narrative in a classification that includes three different types: considering a film as a narrative work, as an ongoing narration in the film and as something that the film tells. Hayward indicates that the interests of the Anglo-Saxon theorists focus on the classical narrative cinema between the 1930s and the 1950s and underlines that oedipal narratives are dominant in these narratives. Narratives are explained by the order/disorder/new order and order/riddle/solution trilogies. These trilogies repeat the patriarchal society's discourse by following the male character's successful or unsuccessful completion of the oedipal orbit (Hayward, 2012: 44–45). Gerard Genette reveals his thoughts about narrative and narratology by stating that there is a vagueness in the word narrative. The narrative is expressed as a verbal or written discourse that undertakes to describe an event or a series of events. The narrative content, on the other hand, refers to a series of real or fictitious events that constitute the themes of discourse from the point of view of theorists and their relationships such as attachment, contrast, repetition etc. According to Genette, therefore, the narrative analysis is explained as an examination by leaving aside the integrity of actions and situations and the linguistic or other means which ensure that the knowledge of this integrity reaches the reader. The third meaning of the narrative is the reference to an event that occurs as a result of someone conveying something, not the event being conveyed while referring to an event (Genette, 2011: 13). According to Jose Angel Garcia Landa and Susan Onega, the narrative is a semiotic representation of a series of events that are temporally and causally related in a meaningful way. In the narrow sense, it is determined by the presence of a narrator and a verbal text (Landa, Onega, 2002: 12). The most important question that Landa and Onega questioned in terms of the scientists of the narrative is: "in what sense can we analyze the structure of the narrative?" Landa and Onega indicate that the narrative is a combination and that this combination can be analyzed in more than one way. If the narrative is the representation in the series of events, the structure of the representation is examined in the analysis. In this regard, the level of analysis of each theorist also includes differences (Landa, Onega, 2002: 14–15).

The Russian formalist and the folk scientist Propp presented his ideas on how tales were handled while examining and his ideas have been accepted as the trivet that constitutes one of the basic pillars of narratology. According to Propp, the examination of fairy tales is in many respects comparable to the study of organic forms in nature. It deals with the types and kinds of phenomena that are identical in essence like the folklorist and the naturalist. Propp classified the narrators of the tales and the items in the fairy tale both in terms of the examination of tales. According to Propp, the functions of the narrative persons can be distinguished, and in extraordinary tales, there are thirty-one of these functions.

The total number of items in the tale and the formative sections are indicated as approximately one-hundred-and-fifty. Each of these elements is named according to its role in the flow of the action (Todorov, 2016: 220–222). But what is the historical origin of the characters that give life to these narratives? Where did the characters come from? When the directors bring the characters to life, which characters have they seen in their lives before? These are the basic questions that every narrative scientist should ask. Narratives may come from legends, and characters may have come from legends. Therefore, it is necessary to know that the story of the characters is also a subject of examination.

In his book *The Hero's Journey* (1949), mythologist Joseph Campbell indicates that the mythological story of the hero is presented with a monomyth sketch. In the mythological adventure of the character, there are monomyth core units classified as separation, maturation, and return. While reinforcing these units with a scheme and mythological examples, Campbell also presents the development of events when he tells what the character encounters in the story (Campbell, 2017: 35). According to Campbell, changes in the monomyth scale are accepted to be beyond description. Different characters or chapters can blend, or a single element can replicate itself. Campbell states that the outlines of myths and stories can get harmed in this context (Campbell, 2017: 222). While structuralists who reveal the basic building blocks of narratology provide the analysis of narratives in various ways, they also provide an understanding of the characters. As a theoretician who presents sources to narratology, Roland Barthes makes detailed explanations of the methods and his analyses form the basis with regard to narratology.

Barthes is an important source in terms of narrative analysis as a person who provides the development of semiotics and text theory. Barthes indicates that in the structural analysis of the narrative, Russian formalism (1920–1925) consisted of poets, literary critics, linguists and folklorists who worked on the forms of which the works took. According to him, Tzvetan Todorov and Vladimir Propp are the prominent Russian formalists. Barthes thinks that Claude Levi Strauss and Algirdas Julien Greimas are also important theorists who bring new innovations to narrative analysis in terms of methodology. Barthes adds that he considers important the works of the semiology-linguistic community run by Greimas in the Center D'etudes des Communications de Masse (Mass Media Research Center) of the École Pratique des Hautes Études. Barthes points out that the French structuralists Jacques Derrida, Jacques Lacan and Louis Althusser are important theorists for the ideas they brought to the structural analysis of the narrative and there are deep ideological differences among these theorists (Barthes, 2016: 145–148). By looking at the example of how the researchers working on the neurophysiology of seeing structuralism explain the subject matter, Claude Levi Strauss exemplifies how he explains the subject. According to Strauss, although the solution of the problem of experience/mind opposition seems to lie in the structure of the nervous system, the solution is the form of the formation of the nervous system and somewhere between the mind and experience. In other words, according to Strauss, structuralists are the ones who researched the invariant elements between the unchanging and differences on the surface (Strauss, 2018: 27–28). According to Todorov, structuralism attaches great importance to the theoretical discourse, and in the literary research, it puts more emphasis on the theory than the annotation (Todorov, 2014: 24). For Todorov, the semantic appearance of the text is the meaning of the work. Therefore, from the point of view of Todorov, when discussing the semantic view of the text, the purpose of these discussions is not to alter the meaning of the work, but only to present and systematize (Todorov, 2014: 47). Todorov's explanations clarify why, in literary research, the theory is prioritized as compared to the annotation.

The systems of thought put forward by the structuralists allow the opening of paradigms of abstract thinking and can sometimes provide very tangible data in understanding the film narratives. According to Robert Stam, structuralism is a method rather than a doctrine, and it deals with immanent relationships that make up all discursive systems (Stam, 2014: 116).

Mehmet Rifat, who is one of the most important Turkish theorists working on the theories of structuralists and in the relevant fields of semiotics and linguistics, and his work *Twentieth-Century Theories of Semiotics and Linguistics* (1983) can be considered as an important literature source in the Turkish academic literature. In his work, Rifat explains in detail the theorists who have contributed to the formation of the basis of narratology. In his book, Rifat mentions the following names: Ferdinand de Saussure, Antoine Millet, Roman Jakobson, Andre Martinet, Noam Chomsky, Otto Jespersen, Gustave Guillaume, Lucien Tesniere, Emile Benveniste, Bernard Pottier, the School of Linguistics in Geneva, the circle of linguistics in Prague, the circle of linguistics in Copenhagen, American structuralism, functional linguistics and Paris Semiology School (Rifat, 1990). Structuralists have played an important role in the foundation of narratology. Narratology, which has been developed over the years and has been studied in different fields, has become an area where many theorists offer their contributions as an interdisciplinary study theory. In this context, understanding the ideas of structuralists is important for understanding the essentials of narratology.

Jahn summarizes the theorists who have contributed to narratology, along with their fields: Psychoanalysis and Storytelling, Peter Brooks, Reading for the Plot: Design and Intention in Narrative – 1984; Narrative Based on Historiography, I doze and wake: The Deviance of Simultaneous Narration, Dorrit Cohn – 1999; Narrative of Possible Worlds, Marie Laure Ryan, Artificial Intelligence and Narrative Theory – 1991; Postmodernism and Doctrine of Panfictionality – 1998; Space in Fiction, Ruth Ronen – 1994; Andrea Gutenberg-Mögliche Welten: Plot und Sinnstiftung im Englischen Frauenroman – 2000; Law's Stories: Narrative and Rhetoric in the Law, Peter Brooks and Paul Gewirtz – 1996; Feminist Narratology, The Narrative Act: Prose Fiction, Susan Lanser – 1992; Ambiguous Discourse: Feminist Narratology and British Women Writers, Kathy Mezei – 1996; Gender Research Narrative Ansgar Nünning, Expositional Modes and Temporal Ordering in Fiction, Meir Sternberg – 1993; Windows of Focalization: Deconstructing and Reconstructing Narratological Concept, Manfred Jahn – 1997; Second Person Fiction: Narrative "You" As Addressee And/Or Protagonist, Monica Fludernik – 1993; Freehand Discourse: A Survey of Recent Accounts, Brian McHale – 1987; Postmodernist Fiction, 1992; Postmodern Narrative Theory, Mark Curie – 1998, Narrative as Rhetoric, Phelan – 1996; Rhetorical Narratology, Kearns – 1999, Cultural Studies Narratology, Nünning – 2000, Transgeneric Narratology, Towards a Cultural and Historical Narratology: A Survey of Diachronic Approaches, Concepts and Research Projects, Ansgar-Vera Nünning – 2002; Transgeneric Narratology: Applications of Lyric Poetry, Prof. Dr. Peter Hühn – 2004; Political Narratology, Mieke Bal – 2004; On Story-Telling: Essays in Narratology, Mieke Bal – 2004, Psychonarratology, Marisa Bortolussi and Peter Dixon; Psychonarratology Foundations for the

Empirical Study of Literary Response, Marisa Bortolussi and Peter Dixon – 2003. Jahn adds that the researchers of the present day emphasize that the discipline of narratology is open to sciences especially like linguistics, cognitive sciences, artificial intelligence and pragmatics / pragmatic science (Jahn, 2015: 46). The ideas of the theorists who explain their ideas in the field of narratology also play an important role in the study of film narratives. Since the film narratives can be studied with a variety of analysis methods, the ideas of all these theorists can be used. In this context, cinema is important in terms of internalizing theories and approaches as an interdisciplinary field.

Narratology Elements in Film Narratives

The different approaches of David Bordwell, Kristin Thompson and Seymour Chatman in understanding narratology elements with regard to film narratives provide explanatory information about which meanings the used concepts contain. As the information of the aforementioned theorists regarding the elements of the narrative will be used as the base in the examinations in this book, especially the concepts and ideas of these theorists are explained.

While the film narratives are built on the plot, narratology questions the foundation of this construction and solve the language of narrative strategies in cinema. The subject of how the construction process is realized reveals the differences in classical cinema narrative or contemporary narrative cinema. Because, in both film narratives, the creation order and discourses of film narrative are different. In this respect, it is possible to indicate that the concept of film style informs the spectator about the way and the layout in which the film is created. The style of the film is based on the principles of the organization that will activate the elements of film techniques. The film style concept is also used to determine the repetitive properties of the structure or to specify the properties of the body of the film. Style and syuzhet affect each other in various ways in the plan in the story (Bordwell, 1985: 50). In this context, it is primarily important to make sense of what the elements of the narrative mean, likewise, with regard to understanding the difference between classical cinema narratives and contemporary narrative cinema, the elements related to the narrative should be internalized.

The plot and story elements that make up the narrative reveal the most important clues about making sense of how the narrative is constructed and presented to the spectator.

Bordwell and Thompson state that a series of events within the narrative that are clearly shown or that are directly understood by the spectators constitute the story. All the story events that are directly defined are included in the plot. The plot clearly shows specific story events, both of which belong to the story and to the plot. The story, on the other hand, goes beyond the plot by implying some unwitnessed diegetic events (Bordwell and Thompson, 2012: 80–81). Some theoreticians prefer to use the concepts of fabula and syuzhet when explaining or examining narratives. Bordwell points out that fabula materializes events in a chronological way in the cause and effect chain at a given time and in a spatial field. Thus, fabula composes a model for making inferences and assumptions with regard to the people who perceive the narrative (Bordwell, 1985: 49). Syuzhet (usually translated as plot) means the presentation and actual arrangement of fabula in the film. Although it has a more abstract construction, it provides the patterning of the story in detail and in an order. Todorov states that Viktor Borisovich Shklovsky, one of the pioneers of the school of Russian formalism, explains the distinction between syuzhet and fabula as follows: "the concept of syuzhet (subject) often interferes with the description of events and what I propose to define as fabula. In fact, fabula is merely a tool for the creation of the subject" (Todorov, 2016: 51). Another important figure of Russian formalism Boris Viktorovich Tomashevsky indicates that fabula and the subject are different concepts. He summarizes the matter by stating that the subject is composed of the same events as the fabula, but the subject follows the sequence of events occurring in the artwork and the sequence of information indicating them. He indicates that fabula, on the other hand, pragmatically can be given in the natural order, that is, irrespective of the way the events are organized in the artwork, according to their causal and chronological order. In brief, fabula is described as a whole of events that are connected to each other and conveyed to the reader throughout the work (Todorov, 2016: 251–252). While Tomashevsky speaks of fabula and syuzhet at the level of analysis of the narrative, Bal says that the narrative has three basic levels of analysis; fabula, story and text. While Fabula is described as everything that happens to the character, the story is expressed as a specific way of transferring the action in the space (Landa and Onega, 2002: 15–16).

Chatman described the story in two parts as a chain of content or events, and a discourse, in other words, an expression with them (i.e. characters, time, and elements of space). The story shows the 'what' of the narrative and the discourse shows the 'how' of the narrative (Chatman, 2009: 17). While the story is expressed as the content of the narrative expression, the discourse is defined as the form of the expression (Chatman, 2009: 21). The formal content element of the narrative that is communicated is the story and it communicates through discourse and the formal expression element. Discourse expresses the story in two ways: continuous and static. While the continuous discourse occurs when someone does something, static discourse is about what happens in the story (Chatman, 2009: 28). In the film reviews in the book, the expression is provided in cinematic language by using the concepts of story and plot. The story and plot reveal the narrative strategies of the films in their connection with character and time elements as the backbone elements of film narrative. In this context, the narrator element becomes important as well. According to Booth, in each reading experience, there is an implicit dialogue between the writer, narrator, other characters and the reader. These four elements relate to each other in different ways, from moral or intellectual, aesthetic and physical identification to opposing. Booth says, "when the elements that are discussed as aesthetic distance come into play here, distance in time and space, social class, speaking or dressing help to control the feeling that we are dealing with an aesthetic object". He likens this situation to the alienating effect of paper months and other unreal scene effects in the modern theater (Booth, 2012: 168). The element that Booth describes as the reader can be read as the spectator in cinema. The narrator is the director and the writer is the scriptwriter. However, it is important to note that the director and the scriptwriter may be the same person. The author, who is described as implicit, is the implied author and the reader should understand that this author is the implied person. Many of the stage effects that can appear in modern theater are already used in cinema, and even cinema borrows many narrative strategies from the theater.

The spectator element is an element that complements the narrative as one of the main components of the narrative. According to the narrative structure of the narrative, the spectator can either be free or can be made dependent on the narrative. The distinction in film narratives is whether the narrative is a mainstream narrative or a narrative outside the mainstream. As the narrative line of the mainstream narratives proceeds straight, the spectator knows how the events will develop, therefore these narratives do not allow the spectator to make deep inquiries. As for the narratives outside the mainstream, the narrative line may be prone and the spectator can never have an idea of how the events are knitted, but at the same time, the narratives in this structure free the spectator as they make the spectator think. Jacques Ranciere states that the spectator is facing an image and does not know the production process or the reality it conceals. The passive audience is standing still and drifts away from both the ability to know and the power of doing (Ranciere, 2015: 10). The spectator described by Ranciere applies to the characteristics of the spectators watching the mainstream cinema narratives. However, the active spectator is in the position of a factor by trying to understand the narrative language of the contemporary narrative structure and trying to solve what is presented to him/her in the narrative. In this context, the spectators of narratives who use the contemporary narrative structure experience the narrative independently of the narrative. The narrative language of the director, who uses all these elements of the narrative, is analyzed in terms of narratology and interpreted with different approaches.

The Elements of Space and Time in Film Narrative

Time and space are the concepts that thinkers have been discussing and adding interpretations for centuries. Both concepts have been tried to be explained by social scientists and naturalists from different perspectives. Aristotle describes time in his book *Physics* in the 4th century BC:

> *"If a divisible thing is to exist, it is necessary that, when it exists, all or some of its parts must exist. But of time some parts have been, while others have to be, and no part of it is though it is divisible. For what is 'now' is not a part: a part is a measure of the whole, which must be made up of parts. Time, on the other hand, is not held to be made up of 'nows'"* (Aristotle, 2018: 705).

Aristotle's thoughts, which allow us to think of the measurability and existence of time, have exhibited that time is a questionable concept philosophically and have revealed many theorists who think about this concept. Adrian Bardon is also one of the philosophers who think about time. In his work, *A Brief History of the Philosophy of Time* (2013), which he explains the philosophy of time, Bardon explains how thinkers have approached the concept of time. Bardon explains that the theories of the nature of time are divided into different categories as a result of a hundred years of work. While idealists believe that time is a purely subjective situation, realists adopt that time is a real thing, a kind of matrix underlying events, and relationalists believe that time is only a way to connect events together (Bardon, 2018: 7). According to Aristotle, time is only the measure of change and the thought of time elapsing without change is inconsistent. Newton gave up the Aristotelian point of view, which saw time dependent on change, and change is now best described as "change is something which occurs in time even when time flows forward". Newton examines time as still a matter of name and as something, although it is not a tangible substance like a tree, a cow or a liquid (Bardon, 2018: 54–55). According to Bardon, the answer to the question 'what is time?' is brief: "time is a 'how' rather than a 'what' and an 'answer' rather than a 'question" (Bardon, 2018: 181).

If time is an answer, then what is space? The question of 'what did the thinkers say for centuries about their thoughts on the space?' has revealed the connection between space and time. The integrity of space and time has also been discussed in the field of physics. In modern relative physics, space and time are replaced by space-time. The reason is that spatial and temporal quantities vary in countless different ways according to different reference systems (Bardon, 2018: 69). Henri Bergson describes space as a concept that is absolutely real and depends on our minds. The space that is linked to the mind is designed as a continuous and homogeneous environment. Making a more concrete and detailed explanation of space, Bergson says, "what exists as real is the feature of things that can be expressed by distance, position change or simply by movement and location connections in space in their ongoing relationships between each other" (Bergson, 2015: 47). Henri Lefebvre, who allowed Bergson's thoughts to be reconsidered, mentions that the relationship between the cyclic and the linear would be controversial. According to Lefebvre, who allows the measure of time, it is the form of the relationship between the cyclical and linear movements of the hour and minute hands. Lefebvre describes time and space as linear and cyclic, expresses the mutual action of these two movements and indicates that he measures them in relation to each other (Lefebvre, 2017: 32).

On the other hand, Albert Einstein explains his thoughts about the concepts of space and time which he discusses in his Theory of Relativity as follows: "Whereas according to the special theory of relativity a part of space without matter and without electromagnetic field seems to be completely empty, that is to say not characterized by any physical properties, according to the general theory of relativity even space that is empty in this sense has physical properties. These are characterized mathematically by the components of the gravitational potential, which describe the metric behavior of this part of space, as well as its gravitational field. This state of things can be easily understood by speaking about an ether, whose state varies continuously from point to point. One must only be careful not to attribute to this "ether" the properties of ordinary material bodies (e.g., a well-defined velocity at every point)." (Einstein, 1918: 697–702).

The ideas that Aristotle put forward hundreds of years ago are still debated by scientists working on space and constitute one of the main sources on which the theorists base. In this context, Aristotle's thoughts about space is also important for questioning them with the ideas of other thinkers:

"Hesiod says, first of all, things came chaos to being, then broad-breasted earth, implying that things need to have space first, because he thought, with most people, that everything is somewhere and in place." (Aristotle, 2018: 678).

Continuing to elaborate on his thoughts on space and place, Aristotle states: "…This is why Plato in the *Timaeus* says that matter and space are the same; for the 'participant' and space are identical. (It is true, indeed, that the account he gives there of the 'participant' is different from what he says in his so-called 'unwritten teaching'. Nevertheless, he did identify place and space." (Aristotle, 2018: 680). The meanings of the concepts of place and space began to be questioned hundreds of years ago. In the studies of film narratives, the use of the concept of space is more appropriate in terms of the meaning of the concept and that is why the concept of space is used in the study.

Time and space express a whole that is inseparable in film narratives. Each element allows for making partial inferences of the film when examined separately. However, the elements of time and space as a whole can show the philosophical dimension of the film's world to the spectators. James Monaco states that in the early years of cinema, the Lumiere brothers influenced the audience by creating time, space and atmosphere (Monaco, 2002: 217). This situation shows how important the effect of the creation of time and space on narrative is.

Since time and space also signify very important indicators in itself, the action of reading each indicator in detail reveals the structure that will lead the spectator towards the whole. According to Monika Fludernik, while examining time in narratology, it should be noted that these three approaches are different from each other: the philosophical aspect of time and its importance in terms of stories and discourse levels, the relationship between the levels of stories and discourse, the grammatical and morphological indicators and their significance in terms of stories and discourse levels (Fludernik, 2008: 608). The opinions of Fludernik on the narrative of literary studies show a questionable approach in film narrative investigations because it is possible to indicate that the opinions of Bordwell and Chatman about time in the film narrative can be addressed philosophically, but it is also important in terms of their level in stories and discourse.

While Chatman and Bordwell's ideas about time and space elements show how these elements are used in the cinematic language, they are fundamental to film review terminology.

Seymour Chatman states that the narrative is the communication consisting of a sender and a receiver. The narrative may be a performance or a text, so the audience is expected to respond it with a comment (Chatman, 2009: 25). In the narrative, events and actions mean what is happening. If the action carries an important value within the plot, the person acting is the character (Chatman, 2009: 40). According to Jahn, the action is a series of events. It is the sum of the events that constitute a plot at the action level of the narrative (Jahn, 2015: 87).

How do these characters exist in the actions of the narrative of the film? Time and space are two of the most important narrative keys that play a role in making sense of the characters within the actions by the spectator. While characters constitute the plot within a number of actions, they are represented in time as well. Chatman mentions two types of time: the time of discourse and story time. The time necessary to read and understand the discourse is the time of discourse and the duration of the events expressed in the narrative is described as story time (Chatman, 2009: 57). Chatman stated that time included events and the story space included beings and indicated that events were not spatial but occurred in the space. Chatman described what is spatial as the beings who perform or remain under the influence of events (Chatman, 2009: 89).

According to David Bordwell and Kristin Thompson, the narrative is a chain of events in the cause-and-effect relationship within time and space (Bordwell and Thompson, 2012: 79). Regarding the time element in the film narrative, Bordwell and Thompson stated that the story time was created on the basis of what the plot presented while watching a film. Events can be presented to the spectator with a flashback outside the chronological order of a story. About the temporal frequency element in the film narrative, on the other hand, a story event is presented only once in the plot. If the plot repeats a story event, it is stated that it generally aims to convey a new information (Bordwell and Thompson, 2012: 84–86).

According to Bordwell and Thompson, space is stated as the place where the normal story action takes place, as well as the location of the plot. The narrative also sometimes wants the viewer to imagine the actions and spaces that are not shown (Bordwell and Thompson, 2012: 90). The question asked by Bordwell and Thompson also allows us to question how the narrative is conveyed: "At any moment in any film, we may ask, 'how deep can I know the perceptions, feelings, and thoughts of characters?', the answer of this question remains in how the narrative presents or conceals the story information to create a certain effect" (Bordwell, Thompson, 2012: 97). According to Bordwell and Thompson, the answer to this question determines the spectator's reaction. Characters function as the intermediaries of cause and effect in the narrative with their bodies, characteristics, attitudes, abilities, habits, pleasures, and psychological impulses. However, all the causes and effects do not appear with the characters in the narrative. The spectator is trying to make a connection between the events through cause and effect. The tendency to think why an event has occurred emerges as a causal motivation. As the plot can provide reasons, the story may not yield results, so the tension in the spectator is increasing. The fact that the plot does not yield results also provides a strong final (Bordwell and Thompson, 2012: 82–84). The mainstream cinema and the cinema outside the mainstream are separated by their own convention. Making sense of the narrative elements, which is the strategy of the director in presenting the narrative elements, is important. In this context, the fact that the films examined in the book are films that use the contemporary narrative structure will require a deeper consideration when trying to understand the narrative elements.

Time and Space in the Film Narrative with Mieke Bal

As the cinema evolved over the years and the experience of film viewing of the spectator differed, there have been developments in the use of narrative spaces as well. Monaco states that prior to the mid-1950s, interior spaces dominated American cinema and foreign cinema. With the introduction of widescreen formats in the 1950s, outdoor camera shooting increased and action sequences became important (Monaco, 2002: 178). Bal characterizing film narrative spaces as steady space and dynamically functioning space reveals how the functions of the spaces that are used in the film narratives have made progress. Likewise, in parallel with the development of the spaces in the film narratives, the time element has improved, and these two elements have been examined by many approaches and methods. Noting the connection between time and space, Monaco explains the connection between the two elements as follows: "the main thing is to create a space. Echo, harmony, etc. or a special space-based 'room tone' is its signature. Sound also produces time." (Monaco, 2002: 205).

The thoughts and elements described regarding the elements of film narrative are important for the internalization of the approaches to the elements of time and space in Mieke Bal's narrative. In her book *Narratology: Introduction to the Theory of Narrative* (1985), Mieke Bal states that the relationship between time and space is important for the rhythm of narrative (Bal, 1999: 139). Bal indicates the necessity of considering the progress of the narrative while summarizing the change of time element in the film narrative: "Events have been defined as processes. A process is a change, a development, and presupposes, therefore a succession in time or a chronology." (Bal, 1999: 208). Bal explains the relationship of the time element with the duration and fabula of the narrative as follows: "I pointed to the possibility varying the time sequence by means of elimination, or of condensation of duration, and of the parallel development several strands of the fabula. These techniques have a bearing on the chronology of the fabula" (Bal, 1999: 212). While time affects the development of the plot, it affects the rhythm of the narrative as well. This rhythm gives a clue about the change of the narrative line when shaping the spectator's causal motivation. If the narrative has a rhythm, it means that the story and plot that establish the basis of the narrative has an effect on the creation of time and space elements in this context. According to Yvette Biro, the way time is addressed determines the tone, style, and method (Biro, 2011: 249).

Emphasizing the importance of the representation of space in the story, Bal stated that seeing, hearing and touching were perceptually representing the space. According to Bal, the connection of the space with the characters enables the 'inhabitants' to convey their feelings to the space: "With the help of these three senses, two kinds of relations may be suggested between characters and space. The space in which the characters situated, or is precisely not situated, is regarded as the frame. The way in which that space is filled can also be indicated. A character can be situated in a space which it experiences as secure, while earlier on, outside that space, it felt unsafe" (Bal, 1999: 133–134).

From the point of view of Bal, space can sometimes get ahead of the story and influence the story. The story is even put into the background in the presentation of the space. The spaces described as steady space and dynamically functioning space provide some data on how characters are represented in the film narrative: "A steady space is a fixed frame, thematized or not, within which the events take place.

A dynamically functioning space is a factor which allows for the movement of characters. Characters walk and therefore need a path. They travel, and so need a large space, countries, seas, air. The hero of a fairy tale has to traverse a dark forest to prove his courage. So, there is a forest. That space is not present as a fixed frame, but as a passage to be taken, and can vary greatly" (Bal, 1999: 136).

The question by which Bal associated space with the character 'how is the space experienced by the character regarding whom space is presented?' provides the rethinking of the relationship between space and character in the narrative (Bal, 1999: 137). Bal states that the image of the character and the image of the space is recommended to be seen by the reader and asks, "who is seen?" This explanation enables understanding the view of the spectator by also considering the space (Bal, 1999: 142).

The information that Bal uses the fabula, story and text trio at the level of analysis of the narrative as a base was given above. In this context, the story item is used as a base with regard to the cinematic language used in film reviews. Before moving on to film reviews, we can further illustrate Bal's ''sense-making level'' of the narrative with a schema.

Sense-Making Levels

Figure 1, Table cited from: (Bal, 2007: 274).

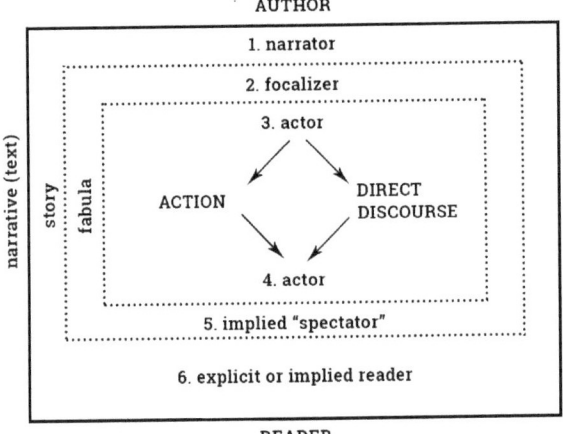

Film Reviews: Space and Time in the Koca Dünya Narrative in the Context of Chronotope

The Story of the Film

The film focuses on the story of two siblings, Ali and Zuhal. Ali and Zuhal were raised in the orphanage as two orphan siblings. The two siblings were given to different families, but their bond was never broken. Ali has the phone number and address of the family with whom Zuhal lives together. But the family does not intend to show Zuhal to Ali. Ali goes to the family's home, who does not respond to Ali's phones and is sent back. One day, Ali stops the mother character from the family and learns that the father character wants to marry Zuhal. Frustrated over this situation, Ali breaks into the house at night and kidnaps Zuhal from the house by killing three people in the family. Two siblings run for hours on a motorcycle and decide to hide in a town. Ali and Zuhal make a house out of a plastic tent in a forestland beyond the town and start living there. However, Zuhal is pregnant. One day Zuhal faints with the blood coming from her legs and suffers a miscarriage. Ali takes Zuhal to the nearest hospital and waits for her at the hospital door. The film ends with this waiting.

Film Review

In the context of the relation of spaces with characters, the concepts of Bal appear as the steady and dynamically functioning space is in the film. The steady spaces are the bed sitting room where Ali lives, Zuhal's house, the tire shop where Ali works, the tent in the fair and the hospital. The functioning spaces are motorcycle roads, forest area and fairgrounds.

In the context of the relationship of the spaces with the story, the spaces where Bal classified according to the motion types of the characters as steady space and dynamically functioning space were determined according to the context in which the characters in the narrative of the film could use their existence on the basis of the qualities of the space. The spaces are examined in terms of the effect of these spaces on the plot. In this way, steady spaces are the bed sitting room where Ali lives, the house where Zuhal lives, the tire shop where Ali works and the hospital. Dynamically functioning spaces are motorcycle roads, forest area, and the fairground area. The tent at the fair can be read both as a steady and a dynamically functioning space.

Bal indicates that in narratives, space can prevent the story and influence the story. In this film narrative, the spaces are located in the center of the story as they affect the story.

The question of Bal about whom the place is presented and in which she associates the space and the character remind how space is experienced by the character and the relationship between the space and character in the narrative. In terms of the relation of the spaces with the characters, the bed sitting room where Ali lives, the house where Zuhal lives, the tire shop that Ali works, the tent in the fairground, the interior spaces presented as a hospital do not take precedence over the story and they are presented as spaces that limit the characters. Motorcycle roads, forest areas, and fairgrounds are presented as spaces that allow freedom to the characters as external spaces, allowing them to behave and act as they wish. Hence, the outer spaces in the film narrative act as a space to allow the movement oscillations of the characters and function as the spaces that accelerate the rhythm of the narrative. Bal indicates that when space is linked to the characters, the inhabitants of the space can express their feelings. In this narrative, the relationship of the outer spaces with the characters is very strong and the moments in which the characters can live take place outside. Ali and Zuhal, who feel their freedom in outdoor areas and who can hold on to life also convey their feelings to their living spaces. For the two siblings who fled from Istanbul to another city on the motorcycle for hours, the roads become a means of escape. Here, the following reference of Bal from Proust is remembered: "Or the sound of a bird suddenly changes the space radically. Space is indicated exactly for this reason, as a space in which the traveler is moving. To put it differently, a traveler in the narrative is in a sense always an allegory of the travel that narrative is" (Bal, 1999: 137). Parallel to the thoughts of Proust, the road is presented as an element that gives independence to the main characters who can travel freely through long roads and who can go wherever they want.

The forestland in the town they choose from the outer spaces to hide becomes their shelter. Forest is a public space, open to everyone and it is a place where everyone can act as he/she wishes, at the same time it is a place where different living creatures live. This situation sometimes prevents people from living in forests because the wild qualities of nature exist in the forest and people accept all dangers if they decide to live in the forest despite their knowledge about the wild. Ali and Zuhal have chosen the forest as the place to live for themselves in order not to leave each other after the great trauma they experienced. If the police find Ali, he will be imprisoned. For this reason, Zuhal and he will stay together for years. Ali would never know what kind of a family Zuhal was given to; maybe he would lose her years later. In addition to all these anxieties, Ali is unsatisfied with his own life and takes his sister to a place he deems suitable where people do not see and cannot reach them. The forested area, which they entered through a town, has been a safe place for them. The forest that human beings would not choose to live easily has been their home. Despite their young age, the pain and the great experiences have caused them to want to get away from people. The two siblings grew up in the Turkish Social Service and Children Protection Institution and they are vulnerable to the ruthlessness of life. The fact that Zuhal was raped by the father of the adoptive family is the biggest factor in Ali's rapid decision when he escaped from the city. The sentence of the mother of the adoptive family "my husband will make her his wife" causes Ali to kill his family. Because of all these difficulties, the two siblings, who have no one in life, have to choose to live in a place that is difficult for people.

As one of the outdoor spaces of the narrative, the fair is presented as one of the places where Ali is entertained. Zuhal also goes to the fairground and experiences some of the moments she has had the most fun in her life and goes back to her childhood. When they listen to the child singer Aytül, it is the moment in which both characters break away from life and look at the child singer with admiration. It is also striking that the child singer is dressed like an adult woman and her hair and make-up are done like an adult woman. The life that children have to experience in their childhood has made them adults. They are children who are obliged to behave like adults by the forcing adults; they are not children anymore. The fact that Ali sleeps with the prostitute who reads his palm at the fair presents the fair as an area of freedom for Ali.

One of the interior spaces of the city is the space that helps the tire repairman Ali to maintain his life. The bed sitting room in which he lives in the city is a place where Ali only sleeps. This space, which has no connection with the character, functions as his threshold location. In this room consisting of young people living in communal conditions, Ali is both unhappy and helpless. Ali does not live in his own room; the room in which Ali lives is a common room where many people sleep at the same time. For Ali, who is trying to live in a dirty room without belonging, this space is far from him. Likewise, in the presentation of the space, it is understood that there is a distance between the space and Ali.

The tire repair shop in the town where they were sheltered is a place where Ali tries to make money from time to time by doing business. The owner of this shop is a young man a little older than Ali. Ali and the young man who owns the shop, try to get out of the troubles of life by going to the fairground that is established in the town from time to time. The tire maker in town is a space where Ali and Zuhal hold on to life.

Zuhal lives in a house with her adoptive family. She lives a confined life within the private sphere. This place not only limits Zuhal but also becomes a prison for her. The house serves as an isolated and confined space, not only for Zuhal but also for the other mother character and young girl character living in the house. The father is the watchman and the manager of the house. The mother only goes out for the needs of the house, while the young girl is always presented at home in the scenes of the film narrative. This house, which is the space of the female characters whose private spheres are encircled, is repressed under the domination of a man. As presented by her father at the beginning of the film narrative, the house where Zuhal was raped is not her shelter.

As an interior space, the tent in the fairground is the space of the fortuneteller woman who creates a private space within a public space. This interior space is presented as a space where Ali experiences his freedom sexually and mentally.

The hospital where Ali brought Zuhal towards the end of the film narrative is a space where both characters are fixed in the flow of life. Ali escapes from the space when he sees the police, and Zuhal receives a treatment in a space where she does not know what will happen to her. Both characters are forced to live in spaces where they were not chosen by life. The interior spaces they live in are not the spaces they have chosen. The hospital can be a space for Zuhal to be saved, but it is also a place that can lead to the capture of Ali.

In the context of the relationship of the spaces with the story, the bed sitting room where Ali lives in the city is presented as a steady space where Ali sleeps only. Ali sleeps on the bottom bunk bed and shares the room with a few people. This space shows where Ali lives at the beginning of the story. The space does not only show where Ali lives but also informs the spectator about how Ali lives. It seems that many rude young people who do not respect each other are squeezed in a dirty room. Ali is a young man who tries to earn a living by working in a tire shop and has his little sister in mind. The place where he lives is like a space where he is temporarily located.

The house where Zuhal lives is at an important point in the narrative line of the story. At the same time, this house is the site of a murder. This space where Ali appeared one night is the death house for a family of three. The narrative line began to be drawn in a different way after this event. The steady home space is also a starting point for the development of the action with regard to the plot. Ali, who rescues Zuhal from her stepfather, changes Zuhal's living space with the murder he committed. Therefore, in terms of the causal motivation of the spectator, the house where Zuhal lives has become important with the occurrence of the murder.

The tire repair shop, where Ali works in the town he sheltered, is also a steady space; the shop has both a closed area and an open space for the engines to wait. However, repairs are performed in indoor spaces. In terms of the relationship of the story to space, the tire shop functions as one of the spaces in the plot as the space where Ali works. It is not a place where important events take place. It is a space where Ali works and earns his money.

While the hospital is a closed and steady space, it offers different readings as well. Likewise, for Zuhal, who is hardly able to get to the hospital as a result of blood loss, the hospital would probably be the end of her life, and this was left with an open end at the end of the film. In this context, apart from the fact that the hospital space is a steady space, it is also a space where an important incident takes place in the context of the relationship of the space with the story and in the context of the causal motivation of the spectator. As it is not clear what will happen to Zuhal, what Ali will do is unclear either. For Ali, who sees the police in the hospital and escapes from the hospital, this location poses a danger. The hospital is a space where the movement of characters is restricted. For this reason, the space is steady, and it is positioned at an important level in the closing of the film in the story. The hospital space where the escape of Ali from the police is shown and Zuhal is intervened with is the space where the events take place but how the story affects the narrative line is also left open-ended.

The road, which is among the dynamically functioning spaces that allow the characters to reach their freedom and to allow them to travel long. Likewise, the forest area that the two siblings choose as their living space is also their dynamically functioning space. The space in which they run, swim, eat, have fun, and visit as they wish, is the forest. They are integrated with the nature in nature. The moments in which they become dynamic by getting out of their stability are the moments when they are in the forest. Gaston Bachelard indicates that the forest is immense. Bachelard expresses that when a person enters a forest which is a world without borders, he/she cannot know where he/she is without knowing where he/she is going. Bachelard tries to embody the vastness and eternity of the forest with the descriptions of Marcault and Therese Brosse and he conveys their thoughts as follows: "Forests, especially, with the mystery of their space prolonged indefinitely beyond the veil of tree trunks and leaves, space that is veiled for our eyes, but transparent to action, are veritable psychological transcendents." (Bachelard, 2014: 225). Ali and Zuhal also experience the endless space while they are moving as they wish in this infinite depth. The vastness of the forest affects their moods and activates them. Bachelard states that the jungle gives out sounds, it is revived by thousands of lives and it also has serenity. Bachelard indicates that the poet Pierre Gueguen mentions the peace that the forest gives, and he sees this peace as the peace of the soul and states "forest is a state of mind" (Bachelard, 2014: 227). Quickly adapting to the mood of the forest, Ali and Zuhal are sometimes afraid of the mysterious silence of the forest as well. But they do not experience the peace offered by the forest in another place and they avoid such an experience.

The fairground area is presented as a dynamically functioning space where both Ali and Zuhal forget the troubles of life. In the fairground, Ali is in the space where he plays games, wins gifts and has a sexual experience. In the space, Zuhal rides the gondola, enjoys the environment, sees the colorful toys and listens to the child singer. Perhaps Zuhal has these experiences for the first time in her limited life. After she got out of the Turkish Social Service and Children Protection Institution, Zuhal was adopted to a family she did not know, she was raped in her private sphere and had a childhood without understanding the colors of life. Therefore the fair can be read as her dynamically functioning space.

The tent in the fair can be read both as a steady and a dynamically functioning space. Although for Ali, who experiences his close relationship with the fortuneteller woman in this space, this is a steady space, it can also be read as a space where he is mentally lost. At the same time, the tent can be assembled, re-assembled and it is mobile. Wherever the fair is, the woman goes there. That is why the space which is steady in itself is dynamic on the other hand. While it does not locate at a fixed point, at the same time it positions at a certain point at a certain time. For this reason, it is possible to indicate that the fair has both a stable and dynamic presentation in its relationship with the story.

The elements of time and space in film narrative can be observed to be presented intricately in the narrative through the concepts explained by Bal about space and in the context of the concept of chronotope by Mikhail Bakhtin. Bakhtin used the concept of chronotope in the field of literature. He describes the chronotope (time-space) concept with the intrinsic connection of the temporal and spatial relations artfully expressed in literature. Bakhtin states that the concept developed as part of Albert Einstein's Theory of Relativity was borrowed as a metaphor for literature. Chronotope, which expresses the inseparability of space and time, which is the fourth dimension of space, is attributed to the formal constituent category of literature (Bakhtin, 2001: 315–316). In the study, the use of the concept of space is preferred instead of the concept of location. In this regard, the concept that Bakhtin describes as space is included in the study as space. Space and time are inseparable from the point of view of Bakhtin. The intertwined state of both elements is seen in many literary works exemplified by Bakhtin. In the film narrative examined, the inseparable integrity of time and space can be read as chronotope. The representation of the experiences, moments, times and spaces in the lives of characters and questionings in their inner world present the reflection of chronotope in different ways. If the relationships between the spaces examined by the explanations of Bal with the characters and the story can be perceived as a whole then the relationship of time with these spaces is also perceived as a whole. The bed sitting room where Ali lives in the city, the house where Zuhal lives as an adopted child, the repair shop Ali works in the city and in the town, the tent in the fairground, the hospital, the fairground, the forest, and the roads change the way the spectators look at the character, their perception in different spaces and also the way they look at the moments in these spaces. The moments in which the characters suffer, or they are sad are linked to the spaces as well. Ali's bed-sitting room in which he lives in the city is a space without belonging for Ali and the moments he lives there are unforgettable moments. The characters may not forget the moments in which they live, even though they feel far away from the spaces they live. Therefore, from the point of view of the spectator, time and space can be said to be perceived and understood together.

When Bal's questioning, in which she associated the space and the character and in which she questioned how the space is experienced by the character regarding to whom the space is presented, is considered in the context of the chronotope, it is possible to indicate that characters spend their time more sadly and painfully in the interior spaces. Outer spaces, on the other hand, remind us of the eternity of time as spaces that allow the freedom of characters when considered in the context of the chronotope. In addition, the outer spaces give the two siblings the moments in which their paths cross with other people. In this context, Bakhtin's description of the road chronotope comes to mind. Bakhtin says: "the road chronotope associated with the encounter is characterized by a broader scope but with a lower grade of emotion and evaluation intensity. Encounters in a novel usually take place on the road. The road is a particularly good space for random encounters. The spatial and temporal paths followed by many different people, who are the representatives of all social classes, societies, religions, nationalities, and ages, intersect at a single spatial and temporal point" (Bakhtin, 2001: 317). Ali and Zuhal choose to take shelter in a different city by passing through other roads outside the main road. Even though some of these roads are not main roads, the people they encountered on this path took them into the chronotope of the road. According to Bakhtin, the road chronotope is both the starting point of new beginnings and where the events are concluded. Time flows into space by fusing with space (Bakhtin, 2001: 317). The road on which Ali and Zuhal went to leave the city for hours is the starting point for them in their new beginning. The experiences they have at the destination and the moments they share with people there indicate the space where the events will end.

The forest, which is one of the outer spaces, is presented as a chronotope of a completely different world. The two siblings take shelter in this space and try to escape from the evil in life. They want to leave all the painful experiences and the tragedies that people have made them experience behind by escaping to the forest. For two siblings who grew up without a mother and a father, the forest is both their mother and their father. For them, time is shaped in the forest. Time has been protecting them. The forest, where people can enter with fear, also includes the brutality and danger. But for Ali and Zuhal, the forest is a danger-free space. The forest is a danger-free chronotope for the two siblings. For them, the moments when wood notes intermingle, the rustle of trees, the sound of nature, the beginning and the end of the night and day exist in harmony in the forest. They experience life just by meeting their daily needs without knowing how time goes by. Some items Ali went downtown and brought help them to continue their lives in the forest. Feeling lonely at the time Ali goes to town, Zuhal is delighted to see Ali as if he comes from another world because according to the two siblings, every space where people live has the possibility to be the space where evil can be experienced.

The fairground where Ali sometimes goes and have fun is not only a public space but also a space for fun. Ali, who has escaped from humans, tries to have fun without escaping from anyone. He brings Zuhal to the fair also for fun and the fair gives them the childish moments that they did not live in their childhood. The fair, which enables winning a gift using guns, sexuality in the fortune teller women's tent, gondola ride and having fun, contains both entertainment and indirectly the evil. The chronotope of the fair carries very different meanings in itself. In this context, Bakhtin's description of some literary texts as the carnival comes to mind. According to Bakhtin, the carnival is the sum of all the different festivals, entertainment and a splendid and harmonious show in the ritual style, but not a literary phenomenon. The carnival, ranging from complex mass actions to singular carnival gestures, uses a language woven with symbolic forms evoking bodily pleasures, and this language cannot be translated into the language of abstract concepts. Participants of the carnival live in the carnival and live as long as the carnival's laws are in force, according to Bakhtin, they live a carnivalesque life. Getting free from the usual codes, this life is regarded as a reversed life for Bakhtin. There is no hierarchy at the carnival, where people are free and intimate and there are free, easy, sincere, friendly, and warm contacts. Strangeness, disrespect, and concrete ideas emerge at the carnival and it is characterized as a festival of both destructive and renewing time. The carnival is not substantive but functional. It does not absolutize anything and expresses the joyful relativity of everything. Bakhtin indicates that the images of the carnival are dual and that these images combine the two poles of change and crisis in themselves. Birth, death, benediction, curse, praise, satire, youth, old age, external face, the inner face, stupidity, wisdom and all of the oppositeness take place here. The carnival laugh is also ambivalent for Bakhtin. The laughing, which is specific to the ritual, is directed toward higher things. It is just as the supreme worldly authority is being taken down and joked about to be forced to renew itself because, in this laugh, the irony is mixed with entertainment (Bakhtin, 2001: 237–244). The fair has a function that brings together all the different elements described by Bakhtin. In addition to entertainment, space contains sexuality experience, drinking, and shooting and presents a carnivalesque for better or worse. The tent, where Ali, from time to time, goes to the fortune-teller woman and has sex, appears to be an illegal and unhealthy environment. Moreover, Ali got his money in his pocket stolen in this tent.

Zuhal states that she did not like the fair after the moments when she had fun with a gondola ride because she understood that her brother likes the fortuneteller woman and she thinks her brother would lose his loyalty to her because of the woman. In this context, Zuhal sees another side of the fairground that looks fun. The funny images of the fair have been bad images for Zuhal. Especially for Zuhal who learned that her brother got his money stolen in a tent, the fair is perceived as dangerous rather than fun. As Bakhtin points out, the carnival contains both a destructive and a renewing time and it showed its destructiveness to the two siblings after Ali got his money stolen. The forest, therefore, reminds itself in the narrative as a chronotope that is sheltered for the two siblings because Ali and Zuhal, who encounter evil when they enter into communication with people, feel safe in the forest. In the forest, time and space are flowing for them and are shaped for them.

The interior spaces, which are the bed sitting room where Ali lives in the city, the house where Zuhal lives as an adopted child, the repair shop Ali works in the city and the town, the tent in the fairground and the hospital, are presented as spaces that limit the characters in the context of the characters' relationship with the space. Likewise, time does not flow in these places. Time has lost its value in these spaces for the characters and is full of pain. Ali is not happy in his bed-sitting room where he lives and in the repair shop he works for. Tinker is a profession that is necessary for him to earn a living. It is not possible to state that Zuhal has a special living space because Zuhal is being harassed by her stepfather, she lives the life of a prisoner and she suffers pain. While the tent in the fairground is presented as a special place where Ali is living his sexuality, it has turned into a place that poses a threat to him after he got his money stolen. The hospital, which is presented at the end of the film, indicates uncertainty in terms of both characters. Ali will either be caught, or may escape, or he will never see Zuhal again. What will happen to Zuhal is left unclear. In this context, the hospital is presented as the chronotope of the uncertainty in terms of both characters. Although it is not known what is expected of Ali and Zuhal in the next period of their lives, the momentum in the spectator's causal motivation is increasing in this space towards the end of the film.

The steady spaces are examined with regard to the relationship of the spaces with the story and the house where Zuhal lives as an adopted child and the hospital space affect the plot and make the line of the narrative inclined because these spaces create the turning points in the lives of the characters and allow the story to be interpreted by the viewer from different perspectives. In this regard, Bakhtin's threshold chronotope concept comes to mind. Bakhtin explains the chronotope of the threshold:

> *"This can be associated with the time-space encounter pattern, but its most basic example is a turning point in life and a chronotope of rupture. Threshold itself (with its literal meaning) contains a metaphoric meaning in everyday use, and it is linked to a breakpoint of life, crisis, turning moment or a life-changing decision (or the indecision that fails to change a life or the fear of stepping beyond the threshold)"*.

Bakhtin, who gives an example from Fyodor Mikhailovich Dostoyevsky and exemplifies that in Dostoyevsky, the main action spaces such as stairs, front hall, corridor, street, and square are examples of such chronotope. In these chronotopes, the time is momentary, i.e. it has no duration and it is stated that it has gone beyond the course of biographical time (Bakhtin, 2001: 322). Ali, who suddenly attacked the house where Zuhal lived, killed three members of the family in the hall of the house. The plot of the story became different after this event, and the time and places were changed. Ali's murder of three members of the family necessitates him and Zuhal to flee the city. If they do not flee, Ali will be captured and remain in prison for years, and perhaps will never reach Zuhal again. The two siblings who have been living separately for years do not want to separate again. For this reason, they have to choose to live in a place other than the city they live in. The lives of both Zuhal and Ali changes in the moment of the murder in the hall, revealing the break chronotope with Bakhtin's interpretation. The moments of the murder are moments in which the feeling of catharsis has reached momentum in terms of the spectators and the threshold chronotope is interpreted for them. Likewise, the hospital space provides another example of the threshold chronotope. Zuhal's struggle against death and the escape of Ali from the hospital not to be caught by the police mark the hospital as a space where the turning point of the lives of the two siblings is determined. While the spectator is left alone with questionings towards the end of the film, the hospital and its surroundings function as the chronotope of holding on to life or being detached from life. As the narrative of the movie is a narrative with a contemporary narrative structure, the film is open-ended. Therefore, the question of what Ali and Zuhal will encounter in their lives after the moments they experienced in the hospital is left unclear. This narrative language allows the threshold chronotope to be read from multiple perspectives and allows the spectator to end the film with question marks.

Time and space present the spectators what characters experience by interpenetrating each other as the two important elements flowing into space. Thus, the spectator follows the events by perceiving time and space as a whole. In the words of Chatman, while the time of the story is interpreted from the spectator's point of view, this interpretation is actualized with the spaces that the director presents. It is possible to state that the interior spaces, exterior spaces, steady and dynamically functioning spaces presented by the director can be perceived in so many different contexts in themselves, so the time of discourse flows differently from the point of view of the spectator. Bardon mentions that the leading character in Kurt Vonnegut's Slaughterhouse-Five (1969) began to experience his whole life in a timeless fashion. Bardon indicates that the leading character begins to appreciate only the existence of the events in his life instead of appreciating the events happen and come to an end and he adds that the character feels peaceful even while he is thinking about the opportunities that he missed and the death at the end of his existence (Bardon, 2018: 101). This interpretation reminds us of the timeless experience of Ali and Zuhal in the forest and the fact that they are not afraid of the wild reality in nature and even death.

With Bakhtinian reading, the film, in which examples of various forms of the chronotope are seen, reveal the possibility of different times and spaces in the same world. Umberto Eco states that taking fictional narrator characters seriously can create an intertextual narrative because these characters are characters that can migrate from one text to another and become independent from the narrative that creates them (Eco, 2018: 162). Ali and Zuhal, the main characters of the Koca Dünya, reminds the novel characters, who try to stay away from the evils in the world, change their living spaces for this, and are filled with purity and beauty. The enchanting vastness and wild beauty of the forest they take shelter bring the other areas in the world to the spectator's mind. The different worlds and the different people of the different worlds that İhsan Oktay Anar mentions in *the Atlas of Misty Continents* show the reader even the invisible colors in the color complexity of the world we live in. Like the worlds of which Anar points out the existence, Erdem also points out the existence of different people, spaces, and areas with the film Koca Dünya. This world also shows the spectator that there will be other time imaginations. Biro, when interpreting Bakhtin, recalls the concept of carnival as a loosening of time, getting out of drafts and intensifying of the rhythm. In his famous essay *"Forms of Time and of the Chronotope in the Novel"*, Bakhtin states that he also calls the carnival "the alien world of adventure time". Biro states that the destructive speed of the action, the vortex of events and the dynamism of artworks do not mean a victory over time and she indicates the deepness of the importance that is attributed to time (Biro, 2011: 255). The alien world of the time of adventure of Biro in the interpretation of Bakhtin virtually marks the world of Ali and Zuhal in the Koca Dünya. In this world, places have ceased to be known places and time has obtained a soul. From the point of view of Paul Ricoeur who works on the philosophy of time, the concept of time should be reconsidered in the context of the film.

According to Ricoeur, time is a collective singular and infinite in size like space. Ricoeur explains this as follows: "The eternity of time does not result in anything but the necessity of thinking all the certain time periods and all the time frames as the limiting of a single time" (Ricoeur, 2016: 80). According to the statements of Ricoeur, it is possible to state that the time in the film narrative is in a collective singularity and infinite greatness in terms of characters. However, in terms of the relation of time with the characters, this can be interpreted in this way in outdoor spaces and dynamically functioning spaces because Ali and Zuhal perceive their freedom and perceive life only in outer spaces. Especially the forest is the place where they will feel the eternity of time. As they live all the time frames in this space, they do not know how these periods of time pass. For the characters who realize that they have passed to another day by the dark, the sunrise, the emergence of the moon and the rising of the sun, the moments they live are the moments specific to that moment. They live in the present, they do not know what will happen tomorrow. The space they live in is the space where they live for that moment. It is unclear how long they will stay in the forest and how they will survive there. In this context, the spectator can see the different times and spaces through the film narrative apart from the time and spaces in the excitement of daily life. The link of freedom in the relationship of characters with time is also a sign of how they internalize time. For Ricoeur, "time is a form of our inner vision: the concept of time disappears if we extract the special condition of our sensuality from the inner sight; the concept of time is not inherent to objects but only inherent to the subject that creates a vision about objects" (Ricoeur, 2016: 80). For Ali and Zuhal, time is an inherent concept to them. The moments experienced by the characters in their spaces make them inherent to time. The moments in which they are inherent in time take place in exterior spaces and dynamically functioning spaces because a lot of things they confront in life take place in dynamically functioning spaces. The interior spaces and the steady spaces offer them the lives that limit their lives. That is why, since they can enter into life in exterior and dynamically functioning spaces and they can be in nature in these spaces, they can discover their experiences in life themselves.

Certain indicators that appear in the film narrative from time to time reveal different questionings about the reading of the film both in terms of time and space and its content. The goat that confronts Zuhal across the forest is a sign of something for Zuhal. Zuhal confronts the goat again at the moment when she loses herself and perceives the goat as her father. Ali saw the goat in the vicinity of the hospital at the end of the film, and when Ali saw the goat, he began to shout "dad... dad... dad!" For the two siblings without a mother and a father, nature has become their mother and father. The metaphor of the goat is like their father, whom they have never seen, coming into existence in the mortal world.

The old lady who confronts Zuhal while she spends time in the in the forest and the mad man holding a mirror while Ali is boating are people who are lost in the forest and who experience the forest except them. Confronting two more people who have lost their mental balance is like an indication that the forest is not a place where people choose to live in. Zuhal finds the old lady dead one day in the forest, covers her with leaves and cries for her just beside her. Zuhal, who sometimes takes the cheesecloth she received from the old lady, puts it on her head, stays put against the wind and perhaps tries to understand what another world is like. Death is not scary for Zuhal. A lot of things in this world she experienced are more dangerous and scary for her. The moments Zuhal and Ali spent in the forest suggest that a forest is an endless place for the characters. This narrative strategy may cause the spectator to perceive the size of the forest infinitely. Stephen Kern's comment on a picture of Paul Cezanne also shows the timeless aspect of time. Around the 1870s, Cezanne attempted to symbolize timelessness by drawing a picture without the hour and minute hands. The still life with a big black clock reveals the questionings of time (Kern, 2013: 64). In the presentation of the time in the film narrative, the timelessness quality of time appears in exterior spaces. Especially the forest space allows for the emergence of this quality of time. In this regard, the experience of having knowledge of the flow of time is also important for everyday life. Kern notes that Henri Bergson indicated two forms in order to know the fluid quality of time which are the relative and absolute knowing. While the relative one is described as the information obtained by traveling around the subject, the absolute knowledge is indicated to be obtained through experiencing something. According to Bergson, it is our own personality that flows in time, and one encounters a series of conditions that contain constant fluidity in their inner self (Kern, 2013: 66–67). Within the scope of the explanations given by Kern from Bergson, the characters in the film narrative experience time both by obtaining relative knowledge and obtaining absolute knowledge. While characters try to understand life through the events that go on around them, at the same time they put up their own fights and thus can obtain relative and absolute information. In this regard, time flows through the constant fluidity of the characters' own inner self. In his book *Introduction to Metaphysics* (1903), Bergson begins to question time and space by asking whether time is suitable for expanding like space. According to Bergson, the reason for measuring time is because it consists of periods. It is, therefore, an impersonal time that describes what is common in all personal times when it is described as homogeneous time. Situations are intertwined in consciousness, and the period is like a widening circle, it is the successiveness itself. Bergson states that there is only a single time period, and the more evolved consciousness is, the longer the time period will be (Bergson, 2015: 49–53). The times that Ali and Zuhal spend together in dynamically functioning spaces and in exterior spaces can be described as homogeneous time. In this context, it should be noted that the duration of time spent by each character can be considered as an impersonal period when examined with the Bergson approach because the time spent in life is a time experienced by everyone, but the experiences of each individual are different in this same time. The important existence of the director here lies in the ability to show spectators the different times of the characters that they experience in a homogeneous time. In this respect, when we examine the film narrative on the basis of the concepts of story time and discourse time, it is possible to observe that the story time and the contemporary narrative structure are formed by narrative strategies. The time of discourse, on the other hand, appears in the bond that the spectators establish with the film in their own life experiences. They may interpret the film by thinking about and questioning the narrative for an hour, maybe they can enter the narrative's time and space by staying in the narrative for a year or internalizing the narrative. The film presents the elements of time and space so deeply and so well with such a poetic expression language that the reality of homogeneous time explained by Bergson differs from the viewpoint of the viewer. In this context, the examination of time and space can demonstrate how the director presents the existing concerning the real and reality in his/her own narrative language which is also revealed by this study. In this world that belongs to everyone, times and spaces also belong to everyone. The exterior spaces that are differentiated in the film narrative reveal the places that everyone can benefit as places that dynamically include areas that are called public spaces. However, the time and spaces that belong to everyone are not open to everyone in daily life. The film narrative can both show this reality to the spectator and present the possibility of other times and spaces. Kern indicates that the concepts of public time and private time reveal contradictory approaches to the number, texture, and direction of time. Kern also reminds that many thinkers, such as Bergson, question public time, which is expressed as a constant and a spatial concept, whether it is the actual time or a metaphysical leak that comes the world of space (Kern, 2013: 78). In this regard, it can also be said that the public times and private times of the characters are presented outside the rules of the social order. Likewise, the characters have already carried out an action that has reversed the codes of the social order by internalizing the forest that people cannot dare to live in. Time spent in the forest is outside of the public time for them. In order to reach any location or to go to any location, they have no time periods to follow. The signs of nature tell them that time goes by. Therefore, they live their private times as they wish. Any small sound they hear in the forest can make the time and space, which belong to them, dangerous. The spectators, on the other hand, make sense of the state of coalescence of the characters with time and space and they move from their time zone to another. In this context, the film narrative for the spectator can be read as chronotope.

While the escape of Ali and Zuhal from one city to another city that they do not know reveals that different chronotope forms can be read, but also affects the rhythm of the narrative. Likewise, according to Bal, the rhythm of the narrative affects the story, which lays the foundation of the narrative, the plot, and the creation of the elements of time and space. Roads are described as exterior spaces and dynamically functioning dynamic spaces and they show two characters traveling to another space. This travel can be interpreted as a performance by some thinkers. John Urry views travel as a performance because, with travel, people are separated from the rules of routine life and develop different norms of behavior. They enter a threshold space where there are norms that appear with the existence of strangers. In this threshold space, new forms of friendship and acting, which can be called temporary games, emerge (Urry, 2015: 36). Ali and Zuhal run away from the people they see on the road for the fear of being captured. The two siblings who spend time with each other during their travel moments make friends with each other and try to make up for the time that they could not spend together for years. The moments in which the rhythm of the narrative is accelerated correspond to the moments that Ali and Zuhal spend in the forest. Although the forest seems immobile with its size and vastness, it offers a space where both characters can freely move. In this sense, it is possible to indicate that the forest accelerates the rhythm of the narrative. Lefebvre classifies rhythms while explaining the concept of rhythm. The rhythm that he describes as secret rhythms shows parallelism with the actions of the characters of the narrative. The secret rhythm is described as rhythms that include physiological but also psychological rhythms (memories, the memory, the spoken, the unspoken, etc.) (Lefebvre, 2017: 43). As Ali and Zuhal move in the forest, they differentiate the rhythm of both time and space. The characters who act as they wish, internalize the forest as a space that gives them freedom. While many actions such as running in the forest, laughing, joking, sleeping on the branches of trees, climbing trees, yelling, crying bring rhythm to the time and space of the narrative, they also show the secret rhythms of the characters. Lefebvre, who mentions that societies contain rhythms, indicates that there are also taught, biological, basic, and pure rhythms. These rhythms characterize many things such as hunger, sleep, excretion, rules of social life, etc. and they are repeated in a linear or cyclic way (Lefebvre, 2017: 71). However, Ali and Zuhal experience life outside of all rhythms explained by Lefebvre. Therefore, the question 'who is seen?' asked by Bal reveals that various approaches can be possible about how the spectators read the characters while looking at them because this question shows how the image of the character and the image of the space are seen by the reader. In this context, the narrative can be described as a narrative that allows for a wide variety of readings both in terms of the examination of space and time and in terms of philosophical readings. Erdem's Koca Dünya is a film that remains close to poetic cinema. The film presents a poetic narrative to the spectators with its images, the feeling that the classical music accompanying the image gives and the way it represents time and space.

Space and Time in the Dört Köşeli Üçgen Narrative in the Context of Panopticon

The Story of the Film

The film narrative tells the story of the attitude of a guard to life who observes in a tobacco warehouse. The watchman character sees himself as an international observer and continues his observations in his daily life. The observer believes that he observes the people working in the workplace by watching them. Observing has been the lifestyle of the observer. The observer, who is criticized, mocked, and squealed to the chief of staff by his colleagues in the workplace, does not give up observing. While the observer, who continues to make observations at the expense of the risk of losing his job, tries to explain to the people around him the facts of truth, lie, reality, good, bad, impartialness, and objectivity, the events in the plot provide the questioning of these concepts. The observer and his experiences in the focus center of the narrative influence the causal motivation of the spectator.

Film Review

The concepts of Bal differentiate spaces as interior and exterior spaces in the context of the relationship of spaces with characters. Concordantly, the interior spaces of the film are as follows: the tobacco warehouse, the storage space of the tobacco warehouse, the cinema hall, the toilet in the workplace, the room of the observer's colleagues, the observer's own room, the room of the chief of staff, the observer's house, the kitchen in his house, the waiting room in the train station, the arcade, the police station, the cafe in which the observer sits, the doctor's room, the office where the observer shares his observations, the theater hall, and the restaurant where the observer works as a waiter. On the other hand, the exterior spaces are as follows: the beach where the observer walks at the beginning of the film, the paths where the observer walks with his colleague in nature, the path where the observer walks alone in nature, the seaside where the observer sees his chief of staff, the open field of nature where the observer plays backgammon with his colleague, the recreation area of the tobacco warehouse, the streets where the observer smokes and observes as an unemployed man, Istiklal Avenue, the street where the observer peddles, the bridge where the observer speaks to the fishermen, the outside of the restaurant where the observer works, and the meadow area where the observer runs away from the observers who follow him.

The concepts of Bal differentiate spaces as steady and dynamically functioning spaces according to the manners of action of characters in the context of the relationship of spaces with the story. Concordantly, the steady spaces of the film are as follows: the interior of the tobacco warehouse, the storage area of the tobacco warehouse, the cinema hall, the toilet in the workplace, the room of the observer's colleague, the observer's own room, the room of the chief of staff, the observer's house, the kitchen in his house, the waiting room in the train station, the arcade, the police station, the cafe in which the observer sits, the doctor's room, the office where the observer shares his observations, the theater hall, and the restaurant where the observer works as a waiter. The dynamically functioning spaces are as follows: the beach where the observer walks at the beginning of the film, the paths where the observer walks with his colleague in nature, the path where the observer walks alone in nature, the seaside where the observer sees his chief of staff, the open field of nature where the observer plays backgammon with his colleague, the recreation area of the tobacco warehouse, the streets where the observer smokes and observes as an unemployed man, Istiklal Avenue, the street where the observer peddles, the bridge where the observer speaks to the fishermen, the outside of the restaurant where the observer works, and the meadow area where the observer runs away from the observers who follow him. All the spaces presented in the film narrative are mentioned above as interior spaces, outdoor spaces, steady spaces, and dynamically functioning spaces but the spaces that will affect the causal motivation of the story are the spaces to be examined.

The observer, who is the main character of the film narrative, looks at the events from a point of view in which he questions and observes life in both interior and exterior spaces. The observer can observe people both in interior and exterior spaces. In this context, the questionings that the story takes to the focal point are closely related to the spaces where the character is presented. Interior spaces like the interior of the tobacco warehouse, the storage area of the tobacco warehouse, the toilet at the workplace, the room of the observer's colleague, the observer's own room, and the room of the chief of staff are the interior spaces where the observer is presented at the space where he works. In these spaces, the observer watches the people working at the workplace and takes notes to fulfill the responsibilities of his job. He sometimes gets a reaction by giving information to the people in the workplace about their mistakes, he sometimes criticizes them, and he sometimes tells people their realities that they do not admit. However, despite the reactions he gets from his colleagues, the observer does not hesitate to tell the truth and reality. The observer, who says that he even made observations by entering the women's room in the workplace, ignores the threats of the chief of staff even when he threatened him with firing him, tries to give logical answers and annoys the chief of staff even more. The observer thinks about what is happening in the workplace in the room of his colleague and determines some facts. One of the most important interior spaces in the workplace is the room of the chief of staff. This space is the space where the observer's character traits become evident, the discursively long dialogues occur, and the events that affect the progression of the story take place. The observer knows that the wife of Ismail has an affair with the chief of staff and even realizes that they develop an intimacy in the workplace. In order to show this reality to Ismail, the observer gathers the other colleagues, goes to the room of the chief of staff and catches the chief of staff and Ismail's wife in close bodily contact. Although Ismail sees all this reality, he wants to understand this intimacy in a different way in order not to lose his job. In this regard, many issues such as reality, truth, lie, ethics and morality in the dialogues between the observer and the chief of staff become thought-provoking in terms of the spectators. The observer does his best to unearth realities in the room of the chief of staff at the expense of being dismissed from his job. By breaking into the room of the chief of staff, who is above him in the hierarchical relationship, the observer wants to reveal the immorality of the chief of staff. The cinema hall is one of the interior spaces outside the workplace and it is the place where the observer opens ethics up for discussion. The observer sits in the seat for which someone else bought tickets, he does not leave the seat even when the ticket holder arrives and claims that the person arrives early can take the seat. The event, which causes the people in the cinema hall to be involved in the discussion and also tends to make the spectators who watch the Four Cornered Triangle think. Although the observer tries to act objectively on ethics and morality since the beginning of the film, the attitudes and behaviors he exhibits in some incidents allow the questioning of events. In this context, the cinema hall is one of the spaces that reveal the personality of the character. However, the observer does not make observations in this space and is in the position of a spectator. After the observer is dismissed from his work, moments of experiencing life in many different spaces are presented. The moments when he takes notes, has breakfast, and questions life by smoking take place at the observer's house. This space gives the information that the observer is a tidy character with the layout of his house, the arrangement of the shirts in the closet, and the organization of the work table. Even if the observer is dismissed, he continues his observations by going to a café or a train station waiting room to observe people. The facts that the observer wakes up in the morning, goes to make observations in the suit and tells the person in the waiting room of the train station his thoughts about the incident he saw reinforce the idea that he is a responsible character. The moment he enters the theater hall in an arcade while walking on the street, he comes across the owner of the theater hall and starts to work as an actor is a sign of the character not giving up on continuing his life. Although the observer exhibits an independent and self-confident character, he must earn a living. The moment the owner of the theater hall sees the observer in the arcade, he starts to talk to him, decides that he is a strange man and tells him that he can start to work as an actor. The observer begins to work in the theater and acts a part in a theater play but makes mistakes in the play that he must not make. In spite of his mistakes, the unconscious success of the observer, who receives great applause from the theater audience, annoys the owner of the theater and he is dismissed again. Resisting to act contrary to what his superiors say, the observer is humiliated by his superiors although does his job successfully. In his statements in the police station after he is taken while he was observing the street, he presents himself as an honest man by defending his rights and not withdrawing from his discourses. Being dismissed from his works, the observer opens an office by deciding to sell his observations, but his office is ruined because he shares what is true about life according to his own discourses. He feels bad about the events in his life, he feels sick and even decides to go to a doctor. However, the doctor tells the observer that he is not ill in terms of medical science. In this regard, the fact that the observer sees a doctor by thinking that he is sick reveals that the events and people in his daily life are in fact events and people that need to be questioned. As an answer to the questions of a customer in the restaurant where he works, the observer tells the facts according to him without hesitating towards the end of the film and by doing so, he clearly shows his character traits without sacrificing his character despite the bad events that happened to him.

The coast where the observer walks at the beginning of the film, which is one of the exterior spaces, is the space where the questioning starts. The coast where he sees the chief of staff with İsmail's wife accompanies the observer in his dreams as well. It is possible to indicate that the coast reveals the thoughts of the observer and it is also the space where the observer talks to his subconscious. The movie narrative is presented in black and white from the beginning to the end of the film, but only the dream scene is colored. For this reason, the fact that the dream scene is colorful reflects the serious effect of the coast on the observer.

The roads in nature where the observer walks with his colleague and the roads in nature he walks alone are the spaces in which he rethinks the questions he asks and tries to find answers to his questions aloud. The open space in nature where the observer plays backgammon with his colleague and the resting place of the tobacco warehouse are the spaces where he spends time with his friends from work, talks to them, discusses and repeats his questionings. While the observer speaks to other people and comments on his observations in life, he continues to question at his lonely moments because he continues to observe people even when he is alone and unemployed. He continues his monologues about life on the streets where he walks alone, on the avenues, on the street where he peddles, and on the bridge where he talks to the fishermen. Sometimes the observer expresses his thoughts loudly and sometimes he thinks quietly. The director used the alienation effect in the moments when the observer talks to himself and also while he talks to another character. The alienation effect is a term used by Bertolt Brecht for theater work in the 1920s and 1930s. It aims is to enable the spectators watching theater play to be alienated from the play. This effect makes the spectators question the play and many other subjects about the play and thus politicizes them. The alienation effect, which is also used by cinema trends, reminds the spectators that they are watching the film in their film viewing process. Using this narrative strategy, the director ensures that the spectator does not break with the reality in life. The spectators have a watching process with both the character's questions and the questionings of the narrative and from the point of view of the spectators, the alienation effect keeps the spectator's distance from the film. The scenes with the alienation effect are usually used in the exterior spaces. In this context, it can be said that the moments of the main character when he/she comments or makes deep interpretations about life are shown in the exterior spaces. The exterior spaces also pave the way for the character to think more. Thinkers have been arguing for hundreds of years that walking has a philosophy as well. That is why the possibility of occurrence of the moments in which the potentials of the characters to think and question reach the highest level is made visible. At the end of the film, the observer working in a restaurant as a waiter is presented both inside and outside the restaurant. After the observer sees the people following him at the restaurant, he leaves his job at the restaurant, starts running away from them and he is shot while running fast towards an empty meadow. It is not known what has happened to the observer; is he dead or not dead? This question is left open-ended in addition to the other questions asked by the spectator.

The steady spaces in the context of the relationship of the spaces with the story are presented as the interior of the tobacco warehouse, the storage area of the tobacco warehouse, the cinema hall, the toilet in the workplace, the room of the observer's colleague, the observer's own room, the room of the chief of staff, the observer's house, the kitchen in his house, the waiting room in the train station, the arcade, the police station, the cafe in which the observer sits, the doctor's room, the office where the observer shares his observations, the theater hall, and the restaurant where the observer works as a waiter. However, since subjects such as the position of the spaces, which are examined in the context of the relationship of the space with the story, the effect of spaces on the plot, the effect of spaces on the spectators and the effect of spaces on the causal motivation of spectators are important, the spaces are examined in this context. In this film narrative, spaces are important as well as characters are very important in terms of the narrative. The steady places where the character makes his observations reveal the questions that the story takes to the focus center. In this way, the character expresses his thoughts either by talking to himself or talking to his colleagues or talking to the spectators and allows the questioned subjects to be reflected on. The steady spaces in which the observer is presented in his workplace are the interior of the tobacco warehouse, the storage area of the tobacco warehouse, the toilet in the workplace, the room of the observer's colleague, the observer's own room, the room of the chief of staff, and the restaurant where the observer works as a waiter. These spaces are important in the context of the relationship of the story with the space because the character places himself as an observer in the workplace by overemphasizing his duty. The observer goes further and claims to be an international observer and underlines that his work is not just a job but a lifestyle. That is why the places in the workplace which allows the observer to make more observations and where he explains his thoughts about the events he observes become important for the story. The observer evaluates how people behave in working life and what kind of movements they have by taking notes, but he not only takes notes but also shares his ideas about the events he experiences with the people at the workplace. The events that occur in working life are ignored and not examined by most people, but the observer does not hesitate to follow the slightest incidents and share the lowdown of the event with people. In the presentation of the observer in the spaces outside the workplace, his ways of behavior in his daily life are presented to the spectators. In this context, the character can be said to be in front of the spaces because although the observer continues to make observations in spaces outside the workplace, how he behaves and how he acts in life are presented in these spaces. Spaces such as the cinema hall where he goes to watch movies, the observer's house, the kitchen in his house, the waiting hall in the train station, the arcade, the police station, the cafe in which the observer sits, the doctor's room, the office where the observer shares his observations, and the theater hall reveal how the observer behaves in life while he is unemployed. The observer, who is questioned by the police at the police station because he continued to observe people outside of work, claims that his observation is not a crime. The observer has opened his office in order to continue his life and to sell his observations, and the people who come to his office are people who do not criticize him. However, a person who says that his observation is an unlawful act also visits the observer in his office. The dialogue between the observer and the young man, who mentions that the work of the observer is a wrongful act, enables the questioning of concepts like law, justice, morality, and ethics. Likewise, the observer asks whether he has a mistake or not, he goes to a doctor and wants to see whether he is ill or not. The dialogue between the doctor and the observer in the doctor's office tries to make the spectators think about the social judgments, the codes of the social order, the accuracy and incorrectness of the rules. The doctor character underlines that it is not a diseased condition for the healthy person to approach the moral events in the social order as an observer. What makes the observer, who is criticized by many people, go to the doctor is the discourses of the people who criticize him and make fun of him. For the observer, who does not hesitate to say what he thinks right, neither observation nor to speak his thoughts about his observations has a certain place. For this reason, even while unemployed, he continues to make observations in steady spaces.

The dynamically functioning spaces which are the path that the observer walks in nature with his colleague, the path that the observer walks alone in nature, the resting area of the tobacco warehouse, the streets where the observer smokes and observes while unemployed, the street where the observer peddles, and the meadow area where the observer runs away from the observers who follow him are the spaces that influence the causal motivation of the plot in the relationship of the space with the story and that affect the spectator's process of watching the film narrative. The observer's walking path in nature with his colleague, the path of the observer walking alone in nature, the streets where the observer smokes and observes the streets while unemployed, and the dynamically functioning spaces which is the street where the observer peddles are the spaces where the observer continues his observations and sometimes shares his observations with his colleagues or friends. On the roads he walks alone, the observer reconsiders his observations and allows the spectator to think about how the story will progress. At the same time, these moments give spectators time at which they can think of all the events and concepts that are questioned just like they give the observer. The meadow area, in which the observer runs when he escapes from the observers, can be considered as the important place in the focal center of the story because the observer is shot by other observers following him. The end of the film is left open-ended in the narrative and it is not possible to find out whether the observer has died or not. Bal states that dynamically functioning spaces provide freedom for the movements of the characters. However, the moment the observer is put in danger takes place in a dynamically functioning space. Although the characters can freely use their movements as they wish, dynamically functioning spaces can be evaluated in a different way in every narrative depending on how characters are represented in the story. Bal also states that dynamically functioning spaces allow travels as well. In this respect, it is possible to question how important the long roads, which allow travel, are in the relationship of the space with the story with regard to the plot. Likewise, although the dynamically functioning spaces in this narrative are spaces in which the character can walk around and run freely, these spaces make the character experience the events that bring danger to him/her. For example, he is caught to the policemen while watching a house on a street. From the subjects that the story takes to the focus center, observation, observing and other related concepts are important in the connection of the main character with the spaces. In this context, the dynamically functioning spaces in which the observer maintains observations can be said to be the most influential spaces in the spectator's causal motivation because the actions that took place in the plot take place mostly in dynamically functioning spaces.

The subject of observation, which the narrative takes to the focal point in the relationship of the space with the character, has been examined in the context of the concept of the panopticon in interior spaces, exterior spaces, steady spaces, and dynamically functioning spaces. Regarding the question 'why have not the spaces, which have been examined in the context of the panopticon, examined in only interior spaces?' it is thought that open spaces may be also suitable for surveillance in the panopticon plan. According to Jeremy Bentham, there are also spaces that are included in surveillance spaces in an open area and these areas, which belong to the building with regard to employment, may be kept under surveillance (Bentham, 2016: 21). Bentham explains the basic plan of the panopticon as follows: "You will be delighted when you realize that the people under surveillance feel like they are always under surveillance, at least it is most likely the case are probably the most important points but that is not the only important point. If that was the case, the same benefit would be obtained from other buildings of any form" (Bentham, 2016: 23). Stating that the panopticon plan is advantageous, Bentham says that, regardless of the purpose for which the plan is implemented, supervisors, all low-ranking officials, and supervised persons are subject to the same supervision (Bentham, 2016: 25).

Zygmunt Bauman and David Lyon stated that the panopticon, a metaphor for institutions representing the state, derives from the Greek words pan and optic. The panopticon, which means a place or a building so arranged that all parts of the interior are visible from a single point, is described as a plan, schema, and architectural drawing. The philosophers, who say that the panopticon is designed as a moral architecture and a recipe for rebuilding the world, also stated that Foucault used the panopticon as the metaphor of the modern power's umbrella (Bauman, Lyon, 2016: 22). According to Gilles Deleuze, surveillance is similar to control societies and societies that spread like a creeper, rather than rooted and grown ones like a tree. Zygmunt Bauman, on the other hand, restricts the movement of prisoners in the panopticon, on the other hand, the guards' movement as a method that facilitates (Bauman, Lyon, 2016: 14). George Ritzer indicates that panopticon is a structure for the full observation of individuals. He mentions that this structure, which is also applied in prisons, is an enormous force for providing full supervision to authorities. Ritzer says that even if the authorities are not in surveillance, the existence of the structure restricts the criminals and emphasizes that the power of the panopticon is increasing (Ritzer, 2000: 122).

Michel Foucault borrowed and interpreted the concept of panopticon from Jeremy Bentham. Bentham's idea of the panopticon is thought to be given by his brother, who visited military schools. In a military school in Paris in the 18th century, students had a cell with glass. All of the students in the school could be seen all night without contacting other students and servants. Although the idea of panopticon emerged before Bentham, Bentham is known as the person who introduced the concept of the panopticon. According to him, the panopticon is Columbus' egg, and it is a technology of power that solves surveillance problems for doctors, criminal lawyers, industrialists, and educators. Foucault explains the panopticon in detail as follows: "It is sufficient to place an observer in the central tower and close a madman, a patient, a prisoner, a worker or a student in each cell. Thanks to the front lighting, small silhouettes of prisoners in surrounding cells can be seen from the tower in the dark. In short, the dungeon rule is reversed; the great brightness of the cell and the glance of an observer captures better than the dark because the dark is ultimately the protector (Foucault, 2012: 86–87). According to Foucault, the realization of the discipline increases the possibilities of power by an arrangement that is forced through glances. Foucault, who exemplified the military camps as the ideal examples of the observatories, states that all power is carried out through a single surveillance (Foucault, 1992: 214–215). Claiming that discipline is the organization of an analytical space, Foucault allows the thinking of the connection between surveillance and discipline (Foucault, 1992: 177). Does observing individuals mean disciplining them? Do the individuals who have been disciplined accept their supervision throughout their lives? Such questions are questions to be questioned in this context because individuals can also be disciplined without wishing to be observed. The subject of the observation, which the film narrative takes to the focus center, can be reconsidered with these questionings.

The panopticon emerged as an idea to observe individuals. Observation, observing, surveillance and all relevant issues related to surveillance can, therefore, be discussed in connection with the panopticon. The concept of the panopticon, which Ulus Baker associated with cinema, allows the spectator to question himself/herself: "A supposed eye, which can see but not visible, serves to form the basic diagram of the disciplinary devices of the entire modern society, not just bad cinema. The disintegration of what is visible and what can be said has become the essence of the operation of everything in the modern world (Baker, 2011: 233). Michel de Certeau, on the other hand, states that the sharing of space makes a panoptic application possible through a certain space (de Certeau, 2008: 112). In this regard, why the act of observation, which the film narrative takes to the focus center, is examined in the spaces that are presented in the narrative have also become important in the context of the reference taken from the thoughts of Foucault and the ideas of Certeau.

The Dört Köşeli Üçgen film provides a rethinking of all these issues, especially as a film that takes observation and observing to the focus center of its story. In this context, how the character is presented in connection with the subject of observation in the spaces that are to be examined in the relationship between space and character is questioned. Answers to the questions 'how are the characters, who are represented in the interior, exterior, steady and dynamically functioning spaces, experiencing these spaces?' and 'while experiencing these spaces, how are the characters seen by the spectators?' are sought.

The observer interior spaces, which are the interior of the tobacco warehouse, the storage area of the tobacco warehouse, the toilet hall at the workplace, the room of the observer's colleague, the observer's own room, and the room of the chief of staff, are the interior spaces that the observer makes observations. In these spaces, the observer makes observations in accordance with the content of the concept of the panopticon. As Foucault points out, one of the areas where power technology can be used is factories, mass production sites, and workplaces because as long as the people working here fulfill their responsibilities and work, the production will take place and the management that holds the power will make a profit. The observer holds the title of a watchman in the workplace. However, he cares so much about his duty that he qualifies himself as an observer and even considers the adjective 'international observer' appropriate for himself. The observer takes notes and put down on paper what people do at the workplace and nobody takes him seriously, even the chief of staff does not take him seriously because the observer specifies what everyone is doing with the smallest details including the chief of staff; he even shares what his colleagues do at their private time outside the workplace when he sees them outside the workplace. The observer believes that this sharing is true because he continues to observe even in the private living space and internalizes it as a way of life. The observer allows the private affairs, lies, and immoralities to come to light in the workplace and he is dismissed. The mechanism of the panopticon has been applied to maintain the hierarchical superiority of power. In this context, the observer is dismissed due to the fact that he has made observation against the hierarchical superiority of power and revealed information that belongs to the holders of the power. In the spaces where the architecture of the Panopticon is applied, the person holding the power is the one who has the authority to observe the people under the hierarchy as he/she wishes. As the observer reverses his position from the observed to the observing party, he has destroyed the codes of power as well. Therefore, he wants to be encoded in the system as the non-existent one.

The interior spaces, where the observer is presented while unemployed are the waiting hall at the train station, the arcade, and the café where the observer sits and watch people, are the ones where he continues to observe. One day, while observing a house on the street, the observer is taken by the police to the police station. With the statements the observer gives at the police station, the fact that some subjects are separated by fine lines is presented to the spectators. When the police ask during the interrogation why the observer is observing, the observer says everyone has the right to make observations. The police charge him with scopophilia. The observer states that scopophilia is the medical term of observing secretly, he is not a person who involves himself in scopophilia and he has the right to observe everything just like every individual. The chief officer of police, on the other hand, indicates that a civil servant's house is always been watched and underlines to whom the surveillance mechanism belongs and how it belongs. The idea that the individuals who work for the state can be monitored anytime, anywhere and they want to be monitored by working for the state is the one that emerges from the statements of the chief officer of police. Likewise, in architectural structures that use the panopticon, employees are those who have agreed to be supervised by their superiors because the seating arrangements and working arrangements are designed to be monitored. Therefore, in the state apparatuses where power plays a dominant role, state employees are the ones who have agreed to act in a panopticon.

The observer also receives criticism about his observations in a dialog in which he shares his observations in his office. Criticized by a young man, the observer emphasizes that it is his right to make observations. The observed young man, on the other hand, states that he does not want to be observed and the surveillance is unlawful. In this context, the spaces with legal surveillance are controversial. The police station and the observer's office make the spectators rethink which spaces of observation can be legal. While these spaces, where the observer character is presented, are experienced by the character, they also allow the spectator to think about the subjects being questioned. Topics such as the fact that the spectators may be observed outside their knowledge, the limits of surveillance, and the content of surveillance in the legal context are the issues that the spectator will consider. While the observer is working in a space parallel to a panoptic thought, the incidents that happen to him after being dismissed for the deconstruction of the hegemony of power brings him closer to those using the mechanism of the panopticon. He is therefore criticized by a young man in his office. That is why the police stated that his actions are not a crime unless there is a complaint but stated that his behavior is not correct because it is the police force that will do the surveillance at this point. No one has the right to watch another person's house. Due to an issue, only persons can be kept under surveillance, and this is done by the institutions that ensure the functioning of the power mechanism. The film reveals the approach that as an unemployed person, the observer can look at people only in the public sphere and observe them because public spaces are for everyone and every citizen can freely use these areas as they wish. However, it is not a moral and legal action to monitor the houses, which are considered as private areas of persons, by others. Even the law enforcement authorities of the state must have legal permits for such action. The moment the observer wants to observe in the women's toilet at the workplace exhibits an ethically disputable space. In all these interior spaces, there is a tight connection between spaces and characters in the representation of the character because while the observer character, who is in the focus center of the story, presents the subject of observation on which the story focuses, the observer character is represented in the spaces that allow the spectators to discuss this subject. These interior spaces are closely represented by the features of characters while the character is represented because the main character, without compromising on his/her ideas and his/her attitude to life, presents his/her existence in these interior spaces. From the point of view of the spectators, the presentation of the characters in these spaces and the dialogues taking place in these spaces are also very important because it is possible to make philosophical inferences from the dialogues on observation and surveillance.

The exterior spaces which are the beach where the observer sees the chief of staff, the resting area in the tobacco warehouse, the street where the observer peddles, the meadow where the observer runs when he escapes from the observers, the streets where the observer smokes and observes while he is unemployed, Istiklal Street are the spaces that can be examined in the context of the panopticon. The coast where the observer sees the chief of staff within the time frame of his private life exhibits the moments that the observer experienced outside working hours, so even though the things he sees in this time period should not be reflected in the working hours of the observer, the observer shares what is happening on the beach with his colleagues. The observer tells Ismail and his colleagues that he saw Ismail's wife closely with the chief of staff and also shows that he made his observations outside working hours. The observer internalizes an approach for making observations as a way of life and that approach reveals a questionable issue. In this context, the idea that every seen reality and truth should be told when it is seen can be questioned because the observer, who sees the colleague's wife in close proximity with the chief of staff, believes that this fact must be known. At this point, the time zone in which the observer makes his observation becomes important. His observations at a space that does not belong to the workplace do not concern the persons in the workplace either. However, the observer who witnessed an unethical event still thinks that he must share this fact. In the resting area of the tobacco warehouse, the observer and his friends talk about the fact that Ismail's wife developed an intimacy with the chief of staff, tell Ismail this truth and force him into the chief of staff's office. This space is an open space of the workplace. The observer does not make observations here but explains Ismail the information about a fact that he knows. Just like every employee who lives knowing what is going on inside the panopticon, Ismail also avoids admitting some facts and does not want to see them. They are the ones who are being supervised inside the buildings designed with the approach of panopticon architecture, who know that they are being supervised and who do not object to it. Ismail, as a person who is suitable for this system, knows that his wife develops an intimacy with the chief of staff, but he does not say anything in order not to lose his job. Ismail has entered the wheels of the capitalist system and he is the one who sacrifices his character and attitude against life. For him, work is more important than anything else, so he cannot hear the immorality against him.

The street where the observer peddles, the streets he smokes while he is unemployed and observing, and Istiklal Street appear as the spaces where he observes life on his own. As he thinks about how to make money while unemployed, he tries to understand life by observing people outdoors. He sells his observations by writing them on papers and people buy them by paying money for them while passing through the street, and this activity is a satire about the subject on which the story focuses. Individuals do not have time to observe in their daily lives and perhaps avoid the observation. The fact that people pay for the observations of the observer is like a proof of how far they are from the observation issue. Individuals who even miss observing life do not make any observations about themselves either. For this reason, observations made by the observer inspired by his life experiences are interesting for people. However, observation is life itself. In this context, it is possible to indicate that the screenwriter who made Salah Birsel's novel a script and the director who presents the script to the spectators with his/her own narrative language have presented the fact that observation and observing exist in life.

In the context of the relation of the spaces with the story, the interior of the tobacco warehouse, the storage area of the tobacco store, the toilet hall in the workplace, the room of the observer's colleague, the observer's own room, and the chief of staff's room are the important spaces in the plot. While the observers continue to make observations in these spaces, the observers are presented in these spaces with the events that affect the line of the plot. The spectators start to question the character traits of the character and the subjects that constitute the focus of the story, and their causal motivation gains momentum with the events that occur in the room of the chief of staff. The dialogs and events that took place in the scene where the observer is reprimanded by the chief of staff and in the scene where Ismail's wife and the chief of staff are caught also influence the spectator's feeling of catharsis. In this regard, when the relation of these spaces with the concept of the panopticon is examined, it can be stated that these spaces are the spaces where observation and also the subjects and events discussed in relation to observation emerge. The events that change the line of the plot emphasize when and where the observations can be made. However, the important point to be noted here is the occurrence of the events affecting the plot in the room of the chief of staff where the concept of the panopticon can be discussed most. The person holding the power in the panoptic context is represented as the chief of staff at the workplace. Many issues such as the chief of staff being questioned by his subordinate and being caught with another woman at the workplace can lead to the shaking of power. Especially in the scene where Ismail's wife is caught with the chief of staff, other employees at the workplace witness the immoral situation of the chief of staff and thus the existing domination of the hegemony is lowered in the eyes of the employees. This situation can be read as the shaking of the panopticon design. The chief, who can watch the employees from the highest point of the panopticon, has become the observed one in the panopticon. Although the observer is tried to be presented as the person with the highest point of the panopticon during the narrative of the film, this position is shaken by the mechanisms of power from time to time. When the observer takes the seat of someone else in the cinema, he does not leave the seat when the owner of the seat arrives and therefore the thoughts of the observer are reversed in this space. While the narrative of the film, which makes the spectators think about the concepts of rights, law, and justice, is conveyed to the spectator by the observer character it represents, it is possible for the spectator to think as a result of the observer's unfair actions.

The steady spaces where the observer is located at the highest point of the panopticon are the waiting hall in the train station, the café where the observer sits, and the office space where the observer shares his observations. The observer can make his observations freely and can act as he wants in these spaces, but because his movements are also limited in the interior spaces, these spaces can be described as steady places.

The spaces where the observer is available to be watched in the panopticon are the observer's house, the kitchen in his house, the police station, the theater hall, and the restaurant where the observer works as a waiter. At the moments when the observer is in the house, in the kitchen, and in the theater hall as an actor, the spectator holds the power in the panopticon because the observer is presented while trying to hold on to life in these spaces, and makes the people, who observe him from the positions of the power, think with his thoughtful manner and questionings. The police station and restaurant are the important spaces where the holders of the power watch the observer. The observer, who is questioned by the law enforcement forces in the police station, answers the questions asked to him and defends himself because this space can be read as the most appropriate space for the approach of the panopticon design. Bauman stated that the panopticon is a method that simplifies the movements of the guards while restricting the movements of the prisoners. In this context, it is possible to indicate that the movements of the observer are limited in steady places, while the panopticon also facilitates the movements of those who control it. In the restaurant where the observer is presented towards the end of the film, the mechanism of power that follows the observer, who has been followed since the beginning of the film, tries to catch the observer to shoot him after he tries to run away. While the observer is running in the large meadow area, the people at the highest place of the panopticon tries to revoke the observer's right to observe by shooting him. The film narrative, which embodies the idea that the watchers may only be the persons in the mechanism of power, reveals that no citizen is allowed to be in the observing position. Emphasizing that the real owners of the panopticon are the power, the film underlines the idea 'observing is for the power only and the citizen can only be the observed one'.

The resting area in the tobacco warehouse, which affects the progress of the narrative line of the story, is a space where the employees gather and talk. In this space, the characters tell each other that they know the affair of Ismail's wife with the chief of staff and think of how they can tell the truth to Ismail. The characters and the main character who came from outside the panopticon are making statements against the panopticon. The characters who try to reveal the immoral behavior of the chief of staff holding the power and who ensure that their colleagues learn the truth disrupt the straight line in the functioning of the panopticon mechanism. If the mechanism of the functioning of the panopticon has been disrupted, the narrative line will also differ after the agreed reconciliation in this dynamically functioning space. The employees come to an agreement in the open space of the tobacco warehouse and decide to break into the room of the chief of staff and in the meantime, they will take Ismail with them for him to see the facts. The concepts of ethics, morality, rights, law, and justice in the construction of the panopticon design have been discussed for centuries. As a dynamically functioning space, the open space of the tobacco warehouse allows the discussion of the issues discussed in the context of the panopticon. In addition to these subjects, the dynamic space that allows the questioning of issues like reality, truth, integrity, and lie also affects the change of the life of the observer. After the chief of staff is caught with Ismail's wife, the observer is fired from his job and now another life is waiting for him. The observations made by the observer at work remind the thoughts of Foucault: "Surveillance is an internal part of the apparatus of production and at the same time it has become a decisive economic processor to the extent that it is a specialized wheel of the disciplinal power," (Foucault, 1992: 220). Although the observer's act of observing functions as a part of the production apparatus at the workplace, his observing the power-holding supervisor contradicts with the logic of surveillance which is evaluated in the context of the panopticon. That is why he is dismissed from his job. The observer, who has stepped into an unemployed life, tries to maintain his life and earn money even though he tries to continue his observations. In this context, the dynamically functioning spaces from the spaces offered after this stage of the plot are presented as spaces where the observer is at the forefront.

The dynamically functioning spaces can be read as the spaces in which the observer holds the power in the panopticon which include the seaside, where the observer sees the chief of staff, the open field in nature where the observer plays backgammon with a colleague, the resting area of the tobacco warehouse, the streets where the observer smokes and observes while he is unemployed, Istiklal Street, the street where the observer peddles, and the bridge on which the observer speaks to the fishermen. In these spaces, the observer can make observations, share his observations with the characters and make comments about the events he sees. The observer, who also continues to make observations outside the working hours, sees the chief of staff on the beach with Ismail's wife for the first time in his resting time. The observer is in a position who observes and interrogates on the beach because he stops the chief of staff and almost interrogates him by asking questions like 'how often do you come to the beach?' The streets, where the observer walks through smoking and observing while unemployed, Istiklal Street, the street where he peddles, and the bridge where he talks to fishermen are the most prominent spaces among the dynamically functioning spaces. In these spaces, the observer has the freedom to act as he wishes and can take long walks, continue his observations and think in detail about the topics he sees. The open space in nature, where the observer plays backgammon with his colleague, and the resting area of the tobacco warehouse are the dynamically functioning spaces that are important for the plot. Speaking about the details of observing in the dialog at the moment of playing backgammon, the observer enters a controversial dialogue with the other person.

The Observer: I only observe what I see, Kamil. Not the things I don't see. You see I play by the numbers I roll, not the ones I don't.
Kamil: So, what you do is like playing backgammon.
The Observer: Yeah but a single-player game.
Kamil: What do you mean?
The Observer: I mean, you toss the dice both for yourself and your opponent. With two players, you can cheat at backgammon. But if it's a single-player game you can't cheat at backgammon.

Kamil: So, you never cheat at observation?
The Observer: No. Because it's a single-player game.
Kamil: You're wrong. There's cheating at everything in the world. From Cemberlitas to beauty queens, cameras. From drinking water to love songs. Even engagement rings. There's cheating at everything, one way or another.
The observer closes the backgammon angrily...
Kamil: Don't get mad. I was making an observation too.
The Observer: No, Kamil. You're not observing. You jump to conclusions based on your observations. And jumping to conclusions based on observations is dangerous. Especially, jumping to conclusions based on your own observations is even more dangerous.

The main representatives of the panopticon are the characters who follow the observer and by killing the observer who runs in the meadow at the end of the film, they make this space one of the most dynamically functioning spaces of the narrative. With their action on how the logic of the functioning of the panopticon should be the characters who observe the observer also reminded the importance of the dynamically functioning spaces in the narrative. Dynamically functioning spaces that allow large movement oscillations are spaces that have a serious impact on the line of the narrative. In these spaces, action scenes can also be presented, as large moving actions can take place in these places. This affects the spectator's feeling of catharsis. The fact that the moment of the shooting of the observer takes place in the dynamically functioning space increases the spectator's feeling of catharsis and an open end is provided to allow many questions to be questioned.

The Dört Köşeli Üçgen is a film that presents the narrative structure of the director and the contemporary narrative strategy. In the narrative, where the alienation effect is often used, the director used the self-reflexive narrative strategy. In the scene showing the cinema hall in the film narrative, self-reflexivity is used with regard to the narrative strategy. Jeanne Allen describes self-reflexivity as follows: "Self-reflexivity is defined as any aspect of a film which points to its own processes of production: the conceptualization of a film, the procedures necessary to make the technology available, the process of filming itself, editing to construct a single presentation from separate segments of image and sound, the desires and demands of marketing the film, the circumstances of exhibition. These processes constitute a film's manipulative nature" (Allen, 1977: 37). Reminding that the spectator is watching a film, the scene enables the spectator to internalize the space where the spectator watches the film narrative. In addition, the observer works as an actor in a theater and in a play in that theater the camera, which shows the audience of the theater from the point of view of the theater stage, reminds the spectators, who are following the narrative of the film that they are following a narrative. Talking to the spectator, the main character explains his thoughts and brings to mind the characters in Godard's films. The poster of the movie Ossessione (Luchino Visconti, 1943) is on the wall of the observer's room when he smokes in the scenes where he is presented alone in his house and this is a reference made to the Italian Neorealism. In this context, the director reminds the spectators of both the French New Wave and the Italian Neorealism movements with his narrative strategy and makes reference to these two cinema movements with the indicators he presented in the narrative. Many features such as the loneliness of the observer, his style of questioning life, an effort for an in-depth understanding of life, his attitude in work life, and his point of view of events remind the characters of the works of the directors of the French New Wave and the Italian Neorealism. Except for the scene where the observer dreams, the film's narrative is in black and white from the beginning of the film to the end of the film and it has been effective in remembering the films of both cinema movements. It is an important detail that the male characters working in the workplace are in dark suits and the women are in dark colored clothes. Individuals working in a space with a panoptic effect exhibit a very didactic attitude in their clothing due to the hegemony effect of the hierarchical power. It is another remarkable fact that the observer's name is not mentioned throughout the film narrative because the observer carries out an action in the hands of the power while observing the persons in the workplace or watching other people in the public sphere. The power assigns this task to some institutions and organizations. Therefore, as the ones who hold the power are the ones who carry out the act of observing, the observer's name and personality do not matter. They were the ones who exist in the space where they perform the function of the design of the panopticon as the ones serving the power; they are anonymous. Likewise, as Bentham says, with whatever purpose the plan is implemented, supervisors and any other low-ranking officials are also under control (Bentham, 2016: 25). An examination of the presence of the observer in life reveals that the efforts of him observing the people in his workplace and getting information about them are similar to the individuals who maintain their lives by accepting to work within the design of the panopticon. The people who observe individuals in the panoptic architecture are those who are appointed by the people who hold the power. As they are under the hegemony, their names become insignificant and the only thing that matters is that they perform their duties. The ruling mechanism can be a workplace as well as spaces like a factory, school, hospital, etc. In the social order mastered by male domination, the ones who hold the power are selected from men. In the film narrative, the presentation of women is secondary as compared to male characters. Women working in the workplace are presented as either the secretary or the mistress of the chief of staff. Likewise, the young actress with which the observer works together in the play attracts attention with her non-speaking character. In the film narrative, where there are the dialogues of mostly male characters, the male hegemony of which the discourses are valid in the public sphere comes to mind. This issue can also be related to the concept of panopticon because, in the spaces where there is the panopticon design, those who hold power are men. In this context, Foucault's statement comes to mind: "a panopticon is a wonderful machine that produces homogeneous power effects" (Foucault, 2006: 298). Men play a leading role in the production of homogeneous power effects and their homogeneous control.

The thoughts of Foucault about surveillance emphasize that those who are supervising are supervised as well: "it is also organized as a multi, automatic and anonymous power because since it is true that surveillance is the functioning of a network from the top to the bottom and based on this network, at the same time this network functions from down to the top and sides to a certain point, and this network allows the 'whole' to hold and the supportive effects of power that receive support from one another to pass through it as a whole: constantly supervised supervisors" (Foucault, 1992: 222). In this context, the observer is in a position of being the supervised one and he is the one who is punished at the end of the film. This reminds the women who are free and who act as they wish in the mainstream cinema and their punishment at the end of the film. The observer tells and repeats throughout the film that it is his right to observe. The basis of the ability to observe is to have this right. Therefore, observing is also presented as a controversial topic in the narrative. The narrative, which allows questions such as 'who, when, how, in what areas and which spaces can make an observation? Can anyone observe everyone? What is the difference between the concepts of observing and supervising?' to be questioned, reminds us that the right to observe belongs to the mechanism of power in the existing social order. The spectator, who watches the film narrative in a scopophilic and voyeuristic manner in the mainstream cinema narratives, is kept away from his scopophilic and voyeuristic position in this film narrative. The supervising position of the spectator is sometimes deconstructed both with the alienation effect and with the use of self-reflexivity. The narrative, which uses the contemporary narrative structure, presents an important film narrative in cinematographic terms with its narrative revealed for making an art film in Turkish Cinema.

The film puts forward the inclined narrative line of contemporary narrative structure and takes the time at which the spectator interprets the space in philosophical terms to a philosophical dimension. In the story, where the focus is the observer's life, the spaces are presented in close relation with the characters and similarly, time is presented in close relationship with the characters. Likewise, film theorists indicate that time and space constitute an inseparable whole. Bal also stated that time is a narrative element that exists in space. A serious tendency is not observed in the time element in the progression of the plot. That is why the spectator can easily view the narrative in terms of interpreting the time element. In the spaces where the events take place, the time is presented in its usual flow. Scenes, where the spectator can think more of the time element, are the scenes in which the main character tries to understand life on his own because in these scenes the character walks alone, wanders around the house, writes notes, goes out on the street and makes observations. Since the scenes in which the character is presented alone are part of the character's effort to understand life, the time of discourse, in which the spectator interprets the film separately from the viewing process, goes on differently because there are no obvious changes in story time. However, since the events of the film and the concepts the film questions will be with the spectator during his/her viewing process, the discourse time may vary. The discourse time, which includes the film interpretation processes of the spectators, differs from person to person. However, it is possible to indicate that the long and thought-provoking dialogues in the story deepen the discourse time. In terms of the character, time is sometimes steady and sometimes dynamic because it flows in a life based on observation. From the point of view of the observer, who experiences a questioning process with the events, the fact that the action rhythm of the incident he/she observes is high influences his/her perception of time. In this case, the moments of action are the moments in which time passes quickly from the point of view of the character. However, the moments when he cannot observe are stable moments for him/her. Especially at the moments when he is alone in the house, the observer is presented as thoughtful and static as he is far from observation. The dismissal of a person who has devoted his life to observing is an intervention in the time of his life. For this reason, time does not go on for the observer in the scenes where the observer is presented at home. When unemployed, the character continues to make an observation and the fluency of time starts for him in the exterior spaces. From the point of view of the character, the moments of observation are read as the moments of time flow, and the moments without observation are full of thought and sadness. The discourse time of the spectator and the story time at which the character is presented are different because the spectator continues to think dynamically about the character's life in the scenes he/she sees the character alone and can be more active in the moments when the character questions some things.

Conclusion

Time, space and character are among the most important elements of film narrative. Time, space and characters, which are presented in the narrative, can be examined with many different methods. In the study, within the framework of the theory of narratology, film narratives were examined based on what Mieke Bal said about time, space, characters and the spectator. Chronotope and panopticon concepts were also included in the study. Reading both concepts in connection with the films is important in making sense of the narrative strategy of the narrative as well as presenting different perspectives while interpreting the narratives from the philosophical point of view. Many scientists of the narrative have identified a lot of methods in the analysis of narratives. Cinema theorists opened the way for the more detailed interpretation of the narrative by using the methods of the scientists of the narrative in the examination of film narratives. As Bal's ideas about narratology can bring multiple readings in the examination of the films, the reviews and examinations were carried out by taking her thoughts and the concepts she used as references.

With the director's poetic narrative, the film Koca Dünya calls the spectator to trace a completely different world. Erdem has proved that he is an auteur with his narrative strategies that he presented about time, space and characters in his previous films. After watching the film Koca Dünya, the spectators met his language again and found the opportunity to question the realities of the world we live in. The fact that the film's story time and discourse time have a very deep look in itself reveals that time and space are concepts that must be reconsidered. Looking at life from the world of children and adolescents, Erdem sought to embody their time and spaces with his film. Ali and Zuhal, who escapes from the evils of life, are the representation of other Alis and Zuhals. While the struggle for survival of two siblings, who have no one but each other, takes place in different spaces, the inner world of the spaces presented is also thought-provoking. The forest, which people see as dangerous to live in, is seen as a place to take shelter in terms of the two characters, while the time experienced in daily life is seen differently in terms of the two siblings. For Ali and Zuhal, time and space are different from the times and spaces that adults are used to living. The representation of this difference is presented both visually and in auditory terms so poetically that the story which is taken as the focus center and the related issues can be forgotten by the spectators from time to time, or the spectator may have a detailed thinking process in the poetic scenes in which there is no dialogue. Bakhtin's chronotope interpretation has a key task to make sense of the time, spaces and characters of this film. The idea that cinema can be in relation to different disciplines, and can provide a path of abstract thinking, has emerged with the film examination.

With the time, space and character elements it presents, the film Dört Köşeli Üçgen synthesizes the subject of observation, which it takes to the focus center, in a good way. The film, which reveals the realities of the panoptic world, questions concepts with an observer and satirical character, and from time to time it reveals a humorous approach. With the events occurring within the plot, the character traits of the observer come to light more concretely. For this reason, the narrative, which prioritizes the inner world of the character, is able to show the issues that the character is questioning in a more emphasized way. The narrative demonstrates how natural making observations is in life and suggests that observation, on the other hand, can be confused with surveillance. The thin line between surveillance and observation lies in the attitude of individuals to life. Surveillance is not a legally appropriate act and also an illness. However, observing is a valid right for every individual. At this point, observation has certain limits, rules, and norms. In this context, how the individual can make observations in which areas and in which ways are examined through the concept of the panopticon. The question of whether the idea of a panopticon, which was started to be discussed by thinkers from centuries ago, is ethical is being discussed by the observer through the film narrative. Sometimes the observer is the observed one and sometimes the observer observes other people. The actions of the character are thought-provoking since he emphasizes that he has not been involved in surveillance but observation, and he does this to justify himself.

The space and time element presented in both narratives were examined according to their relation to the character. The spaces, which have an important place in the narrative, are included in the study and the time element is included in the analysis according to its presentation in the narrative. Both narratives are films using contemporary narrative structure. The directors presented their films with narrative strategies that would break the mainstream cinema conventions. Therefore, with the story taken to the focus center, the subjects related to this story are presented with a thought-provoking approach. While watching both films, spectators may be confronted with a lot of concepts and events that they question at the time of discourse apart from the story time. These narratives, which can change the spectators' attitudes to life, reveal the clues about how the modern narrative structure is presented.

References

Allen, J. (1977). Self-Reflexivity in Documentary. Theoretical Perspectives in Cinema. In D. Allen & T. De Lauretis (Eds.), Cine-Tracks A Journal of Film, Communications, Culture and Politics (pp. 37–43). Montréal P.Q., Canada.

Aristoteles. (2011). *Poetika: Şiir Sanatı Üzerine Bütün Yapıtları-2*. F. Akderin (Trans.). İstanbul: Say Yayıncılık.

Aristoteles. (2018). *Physics. Aristotle – Works*. R. P. Hardie, R. K. Gaye (Trans.). Retrieved from http://www.constitution.org/ari/aristotle-organon+physics.pdf, (pp. 602–851).

Bachelard, G. (2014). *Mekanın Poetikası*. A. Tümertekin (Trans.). İstanbul: İthaki Yayınları.

Baker, U. (2011). *Beyin Ekran*. E. Baransel (Ed.). İstanbul: Birikim Yayınları.

Bakhtin, M. (2001). *Karnavaldan Romana: Edebiyat Teorisinden Dil Felsefesine Seçme Yazılar*. C. Soydemir (Trans.). İstanbul: Ayrıntı Yayınları.

Bal, M. (1999). *Narratology Introduction to the Theory of Narrative*. Toronto: University of Toronto Press.

Bal, M. (2007). *Narrative Theory: Critical Concepts in Literary and Cultural Studies*. London & New york: Routledge Press.

Bardon, A. (2018). *Zaman Felsefesinin Kısa Tarihi*. Ö. Yalçın (Trans.). İstanbul: İş Bankası Yayınları.

Barthes, R. (2017). *Eleştiri ve Hakikat*. E. Bildirici, M. I. Durmaz (Trans.). İstanbul: İletişim Yayınları.

Barthes, R. (2016). *Göstergebilimsel Serüven*. M. Rifat, S. Rifat (Trans.). İstanbul: Yapı Kredi Yayınları.

Bauman, Z. & L. David. (2016). *Akışan Gözetim*. E. Yılmaz (Trans.). İstanbul: Ayrıntı Yayınları.

Bentham, J., P.Watkin, C., Werret, S., Çoban, B., Özarslan, Z. (2016). *Panoptikon Gözün İktidarı*, In B. Çoban & Z. Özarslan. Çev. B. Çoban, Z. Özarslan (Eds.). İstanbul: Su Yayınevi.

Bergson, H. (2015). *Metafizik Dersleri: Uzay-Zaman Madde Giriş*. G. Beşiktaşlıyan (Trans.). İstanbul: Pinhan Yayıncılık.

Biro, Y. (2011). *Sinemada Zamanı Ritmik Tasarım; Türbülans ve Akış*. A. C. Altunkanat (Trans.). İstanbul: Doruk Yayınları.

Bordwell, D. (1985). *Narration in Fiction Film*. USA: Routledge Press.

Bordwell, D. & Kristin, T. (2012). *Film Sanatı*. E. Yılmaz, E. S. Onat (Trans.). Ankara: Deki Yayınları.

Booth, C. W. (2012). *Kurmacanın Retoriği*. B. O. Doğan (Trans.). İstanbul: Metis Yayınları.

Campbell, J. (2017). *Kahramanın Sonsuz Yolculuğu*. S. Gürses (Trans.). İstanbul: İthaki Yayınları.

Chatman, S. (2009). *Öykü ve Söylem: Filmde ve Kurmacada Anlatı Yapısı*. Ö. Yaren (Trans.). Ankara: Deki Yayınları.

De Certeau, M. (2008). *Gündelik Hayatın Keşfi: Eylem, Uygulama, Üretim Sanatları*. L. A. Özcan (Trans.). Ankara: Dost Kitabevi.

Eco, U. (2018). *Anlatı Ormanlarında Gezinti*. K. Atakay (Trans.). İstanbul: Can Yayınları.

Einstein. A. (1918). Dialog über Einwände gegen die Relativitätstheorie, Die Naturwissenschaften. Retrieved from http://dx.doi.org/10.1007/BF01495132, (pp. 697–702).

Fludernik, M. (2008). Time in Narrative. In D. Herman, M. L. Ryan, M. Jahn (Eds.). Routledge Encyclopedia of Narrative Theory. USA, Canada: Routledge Press.

Foucault, M. (1992). *Hapishanenin Doğuşu*. M. A. Kılıçbay (Trans.). İstanbul: İmge Yayınları.

Foucault, M. (2006). *Hapishanenin Doğuşu*. (3.th edition). M. A. Kılıçbay (Trans.). İstanbul: İmge Yayınları.

Foucault, M. (2012). *İktidarın Gözü: Seçme Yazılar 4*. I. Ergüden (Trans.). İstanbul: Ayrıntı Yayınları.

Genette, G. (2011). *Anlatının Söylemi: Yöntem Hakkında Bir Deneme*. F. B. Aydar (Trans.). İstanbul: Boğaziçi Üniversitesi Yayınevi.

Hayward, S. (2012). *Sinemanın Temel Kavramları*, U. Kuya, M. Çavuş (Trans.). İstanbul: Es Yayınları.

Jahn, M. (2015). *Anlatıbilim: Anlatı Teorisi El Kitabı*. B. Dervişcemaloğlu (Trans.). İstanbul: Dergah Yayınları.

Kern, S. (2013). *Zaman ve Uzam Kültürü (1880–1918)*. A. Selman (Trans.). İstanbul: İletişim Yayınları.

Kolker, R. (2011). *Film, Biçim ve Kültür*. F. Ertınaz, A. Güney, Z. Özen, O. Şakır, B. Tokem, D. Tunalı, E. Yılmaz (Trans.). Ankara: Deki Yayınları.

Landa, J. A. G. & Onega, S. (2002). *Anlatıbilime Giriş*. Y. Salman, D. Hakyemez (Trans.). İstanbul: Adam Yayınları.

Lanser, S. (2013). Gender and Narrative. Retrieved from http://www.lhn.uni-hamburg.de/article/gender-and-narrative, 19.05.2016.

Lefebvre, H. (2017). *Ritimanaliz: Mekan, Zaman ve Gündelik Hayat*. A. L. Batur (Trans.). İstanbul: Sel Yayıncılık.

Miller, W. (1993). *Senaryo Yazımı*. Y. Büyükerşen, Y. Demir, N. Esen (Trans.). Eskişehir: Anadolu Üniversitesi Yayınları.

Monaco, J. (2002). *Bir Film Nasıl Okunur*. E. Yılmaz (Trans.). İstanbul: Oğlak Yayınları.

Ranciere, J. (2015). *Özgürleşen Seyirci*. E. B. Şaman (Trans.). İstanbul: Metis Yayınları.

Ricœur, P. (2016). *Zaman ve Anlatı 4: Anlatılan (Öykülenen Zaman)*. U. Öksüzan, A. Altınörs (Trans.). İstanbul: Yapı Kredi Yayınları.

Rifat, M. (1990). *Dilbilim ve Göstergebilim Çağdaş Kuramları*. İstanbul: Düzlem Yayınları.

Ritzer, G. (2000). Büyüsü Bozulmuş Dünyayı Büyülemek Tüketim Araçlarıma Devrimcileştirilmesi. Ş. S. Kaya (Trans.). İstanbul: Ayrıntı Yayınları.

Stam, R. (2014). *Sinema Teorisine Giriş*. S. Salman, Ç. Asatekin (Trans.). İstanbul: Ayrıntı Yayınları.

Strauss, C. L. (2018). *Mit ve Anlam*. G. Y. Demir (Trans.). İstanbul: İthaki Yayınları.

Todorov, T. (2014). *Poetikaya Giriş*. K. Şahin (Trans.). İstanbul: Metis Yayınları.

Todorov, T. (2016). *Yazın Kuramı: Rus Biçimcilerinin Metinleri*. M. Rifat, S. Rifat (Trans.). İstanbul: Yapı Kredi Yayınları.

Urry, J. (2015). *Mekanları Tüketmek*. R. G. Öğdül (Trans.). İstanbul: Ayrıntı Yayınları.

www.ingramcontent.com/pod-product-compliance
Ingram Content Group UK Ltd.
Pitfield, Milton Keynes, MK11 3LW, UK
UKHW021837140426
5217IPUK00022B/1494